Designing Organizations

Jay R. Galbraith

Designing Organizations

An Executive Briefing on Strategy, Structure, and Process

Jossey-Bass Publishers • San Francisco

Figures 4.1, 4.3, 4.5, 4.6, 5.4, 6.2, and 6.3 reprinted from Jay R. Galbraith, *Competing with Flexible Lateral Organizations, Second Edition* (pp. 6, 36, 59, 57, 100, 116, 117 respectively), ©1994 by Addison-Wesley Publishing Company, Inc. Reprinted by permission of the publisher.

Substantial discounts on bulk quantities of Jossey-Bass books are available to corporations, professional associations, and other organizations. For details and discount information, contact the special sales department at Jossey-Bass Inc., Publishers. (415) 433–1740; Fax (800) 605–2665.

For sales outside the United States, please contact your local Simon & Schuster International Office.

 Manufactured in the United States of America on Lyons Fall Pathfinder Tradebook. This paper is acid-free and 100 percent totally chlorine-free.

Library of Congress Cataloging-in-Publication Data

Galbraith, Jay R.
    Designing organizations : an executive briefing on strategy, structure, and process / Jay R. Galbraith.— 1st ed.
        p.   cm.—(The Jossey-Bass management series)
    Includes bibliographical references (p.   ) and index.
    ISBN 0-7879-0091-5 (acid-free paper)
    1. Organizational effectiveness. 2. Strategic planning. I. Title. II. Series
HD58.9.G35   1995
658.4'012—dc20   94-47358

HB Printing   10 9 8 7 6 5 4 3 2   FIRST EDITION

The Jossey-Bass Management Series

Consulting Editors
Organizations and Management

Warren Bennis
University of Southern California

Richard O. Mason
Southern Methodist University

Ian A. Mitroff
University of Southern California

Contents

Figures and Exhibits

Preface

This book began with a request from Warren Bennis that I do a piece on organizational design for an executive briefing series he was putting together. The book was conceived as an update on current events in organizations to help businesspeople choose organizational designs for their companies. The idea was that a manager would buy the book at LAX and be finished reading it upon landing in New York. As it turned out, the book was not completed as a part of that series. But since the idea was a good one I went ahead with the project anyway and the original vision remains the same.

My experience teaching executive programs and courses in strategy taught me that a short book on organizational design would be useful. I was also ready to update my written work on the subject. This book is intended to satisfy all these objectives. It turned out that I had more to say than planned, however. It may still be completed in one sitting, but the flight would have to go in the opposite direction—from New York to Los Angeles—and experience the normal delays at JFK.

Designing Organizations attempts to capture the best thinking about organizing in today's companies. It offers the time-tested knowledge that has been accumulated through experience, as well as the current trends and innovative designs. It presents new ideas—like the virtual corporation, process organization, lateral organization, front/back models—as tools to be used in combination with the old standbys, which include functional structures and profit centers. The book is intended to provide a contrast to the oversell that often accompanies popular ideas. Sometimes the hype diminishes the usefulness of new ideas by turning them into fads. This book portrays the new ideas as useful but limited tools that ought to be understood and kept in every manager's toolbox, to be taken out and used when appropriate. It also tries to suggest the appropriate conditions for using them. *Designing Organizations* is aimed at managers who choose the organizational designs for their companies. It also contains guidance for the internal and external consultants who help managers with their designs.

Chapter One examines the forces that are shaping today's organizations. These forces are raising organizational design's priority on management's list. In Chapter Two I present the organizational design framework in the form of the star model. The model identifies the design policies that managers can control and that will affect employee behavior.

Chapter Three looks at organizational structure. It describes the structures that are increasing in popularity, including process and customer structures. In Chapters Four and Five I discuss the lateral processes, which are management processes that cut across the structure. They give organizations a multidimensional aspect and the ability to be responsive to products, customers, functions, geographies, and work flow processes. Both chapters go beyond relatively simple design issues such as forming teams to discuss different types and amounts of lateral coordination. The structures and processes discussed in Chapters Three, Four, and Five are at the heart of organizational design.

Chapter Six presents three emerging organizational designs: the functional integrator model, the distributed organization, and the front/back model. The latter is a hybrid structure that uses both markets and customers as the "front" and products and services as the "back." This book offers the only complete description of this model on the market today. In Chapters Seven and Eight I examine another popular design model, the virtual corporation. The virtual corporation is a term for a collection of independent companies, all of which coordinate their behavior and act as if they are virtually a single corporation. Chapter Seven describes this model and its design choices and Chapter Eight explains the role of those firms that exercise leadership in integrating the network that makes up the virtual corporation.

Chapter Nine completes this distillation of organizational design concepts by describing the design process and explaining how to undertake it.

In these days of frequent and rapid change, skill in designing and changing organizations is a significant advantage. This advantage is highlighted throughout the book. To achieve an edge from organizational design, management must be able to create complex designs and oversee them. Simple designs offer no advantage and are easily copied. Yet simple designs are popular.

In my view, organizational designs should make it simple for the customer to do business with the organization. Designs should also make it easy for employees with customer and product contact to execute their roles. But if we create designs that make it simple for customers and employees, we tend to create designs that are complex for management. However, that is where the complexity *should* be located. Those leaders who are able to manage complex organizations will attain competitive advantages that are very hard to copy.

It is my goal to make this blend of accumulated knowledge and new ideas easily accessible to leaders who design organizations. My association with Ed Lawler at the Center for Effective Organizations at the University of Southern California was beneficial in developing this blend. Explaining these concepts to Sasha, my wife and businesswoman, helped me make these ideas more useful; her low tolerance for academic nonsense helped immeasurably. My hope is that the reader will be helped, too.

Lausanne, Switzerland   Jay R. Galbraith
February 1995

The Author

Jay R. Galbraith is a visiting faculty member at the International Institute for Management Development in Lausanne, Switzerland. He is currently on a leave of absence from the University of Southern California, where he is professor of management and organization and a senior research scientist at the Center for Effective Organizations. He received his Ch.E. degree (1962) from the University of Cincinnati in chemical engineering, and his M.B.A. (1964) and D.B.A. (1966) degrees from Indiana University.

His principal areas of research are organizational design; change and development; strategy and organization at the corporate, business unit, and international levels of analysis; and international partnering arrangements including joint ventures and virtual organizations. Galbraith has considerable consulting experience in the United States, Europe, Asia, and South America. He recently worked with Institut Pendidkan dan Pembinaan Manajemen in Jakarta, Indonesia, on a study of the formation and development of joint ventures between Indonesian firms and other Asian firms and Western firms.

Galbraith's book *Competing with Flexible Lateral Organizations* (1994) explores management through less hierarchical team structures. His other books include *Organizing for the Future* (Jossey-Bass, 1993, with E. E. Lawler and Associates), a compilation of ten years of research done by the Center for Effective Organizations, and *Strategy Implementation: The Role of Structure and Process* (1986, with R. Kazanjian). Galbraith has written numerous articles for professional journals including *Organization Dynamics* and *Human Resource Management*. Prior to joining the faculty at USC, he directed his own management consulting firm. He has previously been on the faculty of the Wharton School at the University of Pennsylvania and the Sloan School of Management at MIT.

Designing Organizations

1

Introduction:
Four Immutable Forces
Shaping Today's
Organizations

This book is about designing effective organizations. It emphasizes that design is a key task of the leader. It suggests that effective organizations are necessary for competitiveness and that they are a growing source for competitive advantage. The focus of the book is therefore on equipping leaders with the understanding and the tools necessary to create organizations that are superior to those of their competitors.

A few years ago, top managers were not interested in organization, let alone in acquiring a superior understanding of it or skill in its creation. Organization was perceived to be something about charts and job descriptions—necessary evils or bureaucratic activities. Then something happened that propelled organizing to the top of management's agenda. That something is illustrated by the graph shown in Figure 1.1.

The graph shows that most developed countries began investing more of their gross domestic product (GDP) in research and development (R&D). These countries were moving to higher value-added products, while developing countries adopted less sophisticated, higher labor-content products. This phenomenon continues today.

The increased investment in R&D has two implications. First, the companies in developed countries create value for customers

FIGURE 1.1. Percentage of Gross Domestic Product Invested in Research and Development in Developed Countries.

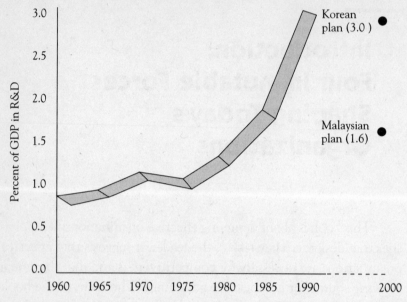

Source: Dertouzos, M. L., and Lester, R. K., 1989, p. 58; *Business Week,* June 1992.

by putting knowledge and design into their products. This "knowledge difference" can be illustrated by comparing the microprocessor with the dynamic random access memory (DRAM), both semiconductor products consisting of equal numbers of transistors on a chip. The DRAM, however, is a blank commodity chip awaiting information. The microprocessor, in contrast, contains sophisticated circuit designs and architectures to achieve unbelievably fast computations, and it sells for ten times the price of the commodity DRAM chip.

The circuit designs on the microprocessor represent the brains and energy of the engineers who created them. It is they who create value for customers in the new economy. So the assets of Intel and Motorola are actually the knowledge and energy of the engineers who create the designs. The ability of Intel and Motorola to compete in the new economy depends on their ability to attract, retain, motivate, and coordinate talented engineers. In short, it depends on organization of the efforts of these engineers.

Second, the R&D investment raises the fixed costs of doing business. For many companies in many industries domestic demand is no longer sufficient to cover all of their fixed costs. These companies must seek additional demand outside their home countries. When a lot of companies expand into other countries the result is heightened global competition. Today, in addition to traditional domestic rivals—those that have survived—there are Japanese and European rivals. In the 1990s it is expected that multinationals from Korea, Taiwan, Malaysia, the ASEAN countries, and eventually China will also appear. These new competitors often play by different rules. They also give our customers more choices. As customers learn how to benefit from the greater range of choices, suppliers need to learn how to respond. As a response to this more knowledgeable, demanding customer, four shapers of today's—and tomorrow's—organizations have emerged.

Organization Shapers

The four organization shapers are the following:

1. Buyer power
2. Variety
3. Change
4. Speed

Buyer Power

The new competition shifts power to the buyers, who know they are gaining power and learning how to use it. As a result, more organizational structures are being designed around customers or market segments. In addition, more initiatives are being launched to please the customer, and as a result they too shape organizations.

Variety

One response to buyer power is to increase the number of products and services offered and to customize them. In order to know more about customers, more and finer segments are created. The result is a greater variety and customization of offerings. To contend with this, management must know and understand more issues. Hence, it must collect more information, make more decisions, and set more priorities. As a result, management must bring more people into the decision processes. Decentralization is the means to do this.

Change

But no sooner is a decision made than the situation changes, requiring that management relearn and redecide. The combination of variety and change causes the company to make still more decisions, more frequently. It needs to expand its decision-making capacity. This capacity is again expanded by including more people through decentralization.

Speed

Customers not only want variety but also want it faster. In responding more quickly to customer requests, companies discover that they can benefit from additional efficiencies. With shorter lead times and cycle times, a company invests less in inventory and turns it more quickly. With these clear benefits to all parties, speed is the name of the game today. Speed also means that decisions must be moved to points of direct contact with the work. Thus, speed too is a force for decentralization.

Today's organizations must be responsive and flexible. The necessary business strategies require state-of-the-art organizations. But it is very difficult to create state-of-the-art organizations. Like most difficult issues, such decisions land on the desk of (or find their way into the e-mail of) the chief executive. Chief executives, like it or not, are being forced to become involved in organizational design, first to create knowledge-based organizations and second to create effective, rapid responses to powerful customers.

Information Technology

Management can get some help in coping with variety, change, and speed by employing the new information technology. Although variety, change, and speed require that more decisions be made more often and more quickly, information technology can enable organizations to do just that. Today's technology can tie people and databases together; the company's entire knowledge base and computer power can be delivered to any person or team on the firing line.

Organizational Design and Executive Leadership

Organizational design decisions are landing on the chief executive's desk because they are difficult, priority issues. And the chief executives are getting involved because they see the decisions as high-leverage, and they see effective organizational design as a source of competitive advantage.

Organizational design decisions affect significantly the executive's unit. By choosing *who* decides and by designing the processes influencing *how* things are decided, the executive shapes every decision made in the unit. The leader becomes less of a *decision maker* and more of a *decision shaper*. Organizational design decisions are the shapers of the organization's decision-making process.

Unique Organizational Design

Organizational designs that facilitate variety, change, and speed are sources of competitive advantage. These designs are difficult to execute and copy because they are intricate blends of many different design policies. Thus, they are likely to be sustainable sources of advantage.

A good example of competitive organization design is the 3M Company. It has maintained an enviable record of entrepreneurship and new business development, even though it is one hundred years old. Many outsiders have visited and observed 3M in action, but few have been able to duplicate its ability to create innovative new products. They can copy particular practices—for example, people at 3M spend 15 percent of their time on projects of their own choosing. But what makes the company's advantage sustainable is its unique blend of practices, values, autonomous structures, funding processes, rewards, and selection and development of product champions (Galbraith, 1982). That is difficult to copy; it is a competitive advantage for 3M. Chapter Two of this volume lays out the framework for designing such intricate blends of organizational policies.

Balanced Perspective

The business world has changed. The solutions to many of today's issues have their roots in new organizational designs. This new priority of organizing is easy to notice. It has been featured in cover articles in the business press, which has introduced us to the "horizontal organization," the "virtual corporation," the "modular organization," and so on. All of this coverage indicates the new priorities as well as an exceptional amount of "hype."

The hype results in an overselling of some credible ideas. For example, it may lead some people to believe that such concepts as *teamwork* or *reengineering* are universal solutions rather than tools to be placed in the tool kit and taken out under the appropriate circumstances. Or the hype may desensitize people from ever listening to proposals for new organization practices with potential. I would like to take a more balanced approach, weighing the positives and negatives of current organizational design alternatives.

I see the choice of organization as a design issue. The design of organizations is much like the design of other things—buildings, airplanes, computers. For example, everyone wants a lightweight laptop computer that is fast and doesn't cost much, and that has a large, clear, color screen, lots of memory, a long battery life, and so on. Unfortunately, a computer cannot be designed that meets all of these criteria simultaneously. Trade-offs must be made. The computer designer must know which criteria are most important. By the same reasoning we cannot design simple organizations that provide a variety of products to a variety of customers on short cycle times and also capture economies of scale to provide low cost. Again, trade-offs must be made. The business strategy should set the criteria necessary for determining the priority task to accomplish. An organization can then be designed to meet those criteria. As a result, the organization is good at executing some activities but not good at others. The leader's task is to help the organization choose. This choice is the trade-off decision.

Thus, any organizational design has positives and negatives involved in every choice. The hype usually glosses over the negatives. Leaders who understand their organizations can articulate the negatives as well as the positives of their organizations. This understanding is important not only for choosing the appropriate organization but also for positioning the leader. The negatives are what the leader will have to manage.

This book attempts to present a balanced approach to organizational design and to describe the positives and negatives of various design choices. However, the choice of organizational design will ultimately depend on the business strategy that the organization is to execute.

PART ONE:

A Framework for Organizational Design

2

Choosing an Effective Design

The framework for organizational design is the foundation on which a company bases its design choices. The framework consists of a series of design policies that is controllable by management and can influence employee behavior. The policies are the tools with which management must become skilled in order to shape effectively the decisions and behaviors of their organizations.

The Star Model

The organizational design framework portrayed in Figure 2.1 is called "the star model." In the star model, design policies fall into five categories. The first is strategy, which determines direction. The second is structure, which determines the location of decision-making power. Processes have to do with the flow of information; they are the means of responding to information technologies. Reward systems influence the motivation of people to perform and address organizational goals. People policies (human resource policies) influence and frequently define the employees' mindsets and skills.

This book focuses primarily on structure and process policies and on matching appropriate combinations of them with the

FIGURE 2.1. The Star Model.

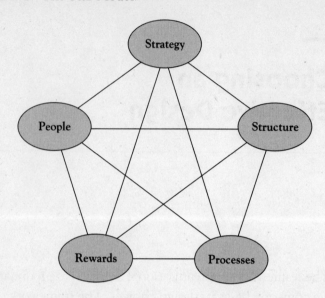

business strategy. The other design policies are vital and integral to the whole organization and will be woven into the discussion when possible, but the reader is referred to other sources for an in-depth analysis of them (for example, see Lawler, 1992). To provide a working familiarity with the five policy areas, general descriptions follow.

Strategy

Strategy is the company's formula for winning. The company's strategy specifies the goals and objectives to be achieved as well as the values and missions to be pursued; it sets out the basic direction of the company. The strategy specifically delineates the products or services to be provided, the markets to be served, and the value to be offered to the customer. It also specifies sources of competitive advantage and strives to provide superior value.

Traditionally, strategy is the first component of the star model to be addressed. It is important in the organizational design process because it establishes the criteria for choosing among alternative organizational forms. Each organizational form enables some activities to be performed well while hindering others. Choosing organizational alternatives inevitably involves making trade-offs. Strategy dictates which activities are most necessary, thereby providing the basis for making the best trade-offs in the organizational design.

Structure

The structure of the organization determines the placement of power and authority in the organization. Structure policies fall into four areas:

- Specialization
- Shape
- Distribution of power
- Departmentalization

Specialization refers to the type and numbers of job specialties used in performing the work. *Shape* refers to the number of people constituting the departments (that is, the span of control) at each level of the structure. Large numbers of people in each department create flat organizational structures with few levels. *Distribution of power,* in its vertical dimension, refers to the classic issues of centralization or decentralization. In its lateral dimension, it refers to the movement of power to the department dealing directly with the issues critical to its mission. *Departmentalization* is the basis for forming departments at each level of the structure. The standard dimensions on which departments are formed are functions, products, work flow processes, markets, and geography. These five dimensions will be discussed in depth in Chapter Three.

Processes

Information and decision processes cut across the organization's structure; if structure is thought of as the anatomy of the organization, processes are its physiology or functioning. Management processes are both vertical and horizontal.

Vertical processes, as shown in Figure 2.2, allocate the scarce resources of funds and talent. Vertical processes are usually business planning and budgeting processes. The needs of different departments are centrally collected, and priorities are decided for the budgeting and allocation of the resources to capital, research and development, training, and so on.

Horizontal—also known as lateral—processes, as shown in Figure 2.3, are designed around the work flow—for example, new product development or the entry or fulfillment of a customer order. These management processes are becoming the primary vehicle for managing in today's organizations. Lateral processes can be carried out in a range of ways, from voluntary contacts between members to complex and formally supervised teams. (Chapters Four and Five focus on lateral processes.)

Rewards

The purpose of the rewards system is to align the goals of the employee with the goals of the organization. It provides motivation and incentive for the completion of the strategic direction.

FIGURE 2.2. Vertical Processes.

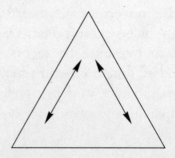

FIGURE 2.3. Lateral Processes.

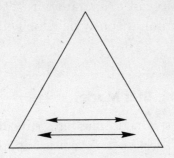

The organization's rewards system defines policies regulating salaries, promotions, bonuses, profit sharing, stock options, and so forth. A great deal of change is taking place in this area, particularly as it supports the lateral processes. Companies are now implementing pay-for-skill salary practices, along with team bonuses or gain-sharing systems (Lawler, 1990). There is also the burgeoning practice of offering nonmonetary rewards such as recognition or challenging assignments.

The star model suggests that the rewards system must be congruent with the structure and processes to influence the strategic direction. Rewards systems are only effective when they form a consistent package in combination with the other design choices.

People

This area governs the human resource policies of recruiting, selection, rotation, training, and development. Human resource policies—in the appropriate combinations—produce the talent that is required by the strategy and structure of the organization, generating the skills and mind-sets necessary to implement its chosen direction. Like the policy choices in the other areas, these policies work best when consistent with the other connecting design areas.

Human resource policies also build the organizational capabilities to execute the strategic direction. Flexible organizations require flexible people. Cross-functional teams require people who are generalists and who can cooperate with each other. Human resource policies simultaneously develop people and organizational capabilities.

Implications of the Star Model

As the layout of the star model illustrates, structure is only one facet of an organization's design. This fact is important because most design efforts invest far too much time drawing the organization chart and far too little on processes and rewards. Structure is usually overemphasized because it affects status and power, and it is most likely to be reported in the business press. However, in a fast-changing business environment, structure is becoming less important, while processes, rewards, and people are becoming more important.

Another insight to be gained from the star model is that different strategies lead to different organizations. Although this seems obvious, it has ramifications that are often overlooked. There is no "one size fits all" organizational design that all companies—regardless of their particular strategy needs—should subscribe to. There will always be a current design that has become "all the rage." But no matter the fashionable design—whether it is the matrix design or the virtual corporation—trendiness is not sufficient reason to adopt an organizational design. All designs have merit but not for all companies in all circumstances. The design—or combination of designs—that should be chosen is that one that best meets the criteria derived from the strategy.

A third implication of the star model is in the interweaving nature of the lines that form the star shape. For an organization to be effective, all the policies must be aligned, interacting harmoniously with one other. An alignment of all the policies will communicate a clear, consistent message to the company's employees.

The star model consists of policies that leaders can control and that can affect employee behavior, as suggested in Figure 2.4. It

FIGURE 2.4. How Organizational Design Affects Behavior.

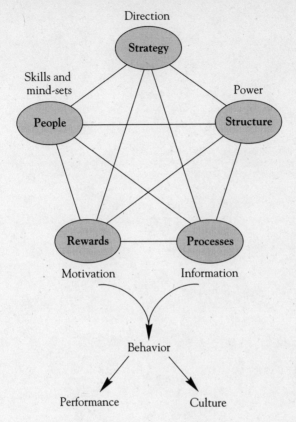

shows that managers can influence performance and culture but only by acting through the design policies that affect behavior.

In the next chapter we will examine in greater detail one design policy—structure.

3

Matching Strategy and Structure

Once the strategy is established, the structure of the organization sets the framework for the other organizational design decisions. The traditional hierarchical structure of organizations—with its dysfunctional effects—continues to fall under harsher and harsher criticism. At the same time, more and more structural design alternatives have begun to appear. There is an appropriate trend away from authoritarian management styles and the separatist titles and privileges of a multileveled hierarchy. Most companies have fewer hierarchical levels. Automation and information technology permit wider spans and therefore flatter structures (fewer hierarchical levels).

The Dimensions of Structure

Hierarchies, albeit flatter ones, will still be around for some time. They are used to reach decisions among large numbers of people in a timely fashion. They provide a basis for an appeals process for conflict resolution. But they are being implemented much more sparingly and in conjunction with alternative structures. Before we turn our attention to these alternatives, it is important to become familiar with the four policy areas that determine the structure of an organization. These policy areas, or dimensions, are the following:

- Specialization
- Shape
- Distribution of power
- Departmentalization

These policy areas are not listed in order of importance. Rather, departmentalization—with its far-reaching ramifications and attendant complexities—is saved for last.

Specialization

Specialization refers to the types and numbers of specialties to be used in performing the work. In general, the greater the number of specialties, the better the subtask performance. But specialization also makes it difficult to integrate subtasks into the performance of the whole task. Today, the trend is toward less specialization and more job rotation in low- to moderate-skill tasks in order to allow speed and ease of coordination while in high-skill tasks the trend is toward greater specialization in order to allow pursuit of in-depth knowledge.

The old rules of the division of labor were to break tasks into subtasks and have people specialize in small pieces of the work. For complex tasks, the work could be divided so that an expert could bring in-depth knowledge to bear on difficult issues. Electrical engineering work was broken into electromechanical and electronics segments. The electronics segment could be further divided, down to the role of circuit designer for digital signal processing.

A different logic applied to the subdivision of low-skill tasks. Work was divided to create simple tasks so that uneducated workers could perform them at low wages. Such workers were easy to find and little training was needed. If turnover was high, new workers could be found and made productive at little expense. This thinking still applies in developing countries.

But in developed countries, the old logic still applies only for complex, high-technology work. Companies in electronics, genetics, and pharmaceuticals all search for experts in specialized fields to push the limits of technology. The level of specialization is actually increasing as new specialties are created every day. Specialization of high-skill workers allows talented employees to gain greater expertise in their specific areas. The expertise can often be accumulated into databases and delivered to the teams by new information devices. These devices provide text, graphics, photos, and video to teach multiskilled workers. Thus, the expertise not only serves its primary purpose of allowing the specialist to gain in-depth knowledge but also can be disseminated to educate and inform generalists.

In contrast, at the low- and medium-skill levels, several forces are combining to eliminate highly fragmented tasks. Simple low-skill tasks are being automated (machines can do the tasks more cheaply and reliably than people can) or exported to developing countries. In addition, the costs of coordinating fragmented, interdependent tasks are too high in rapidly changing situations; a large amount of communication is needed to combine the work when hundreds of subtasks are involved. The remaining low- and moderate-skill work is being handled by multiskilled teams of educated workers. These teams are given end-to-end responsibility to make decisions for an entire piece of work, providing a more rapid and effective work flow.

These new work arrangements offer the benefits of greater speed and motivation and lower coordination costs (see Lawler, 1986).

Shape

Shape is determined by the number of people forming departments at each hierarchical level. The more people per department, the fewer the levels. The number of people in a department is usually referred to as the span of control—or span of supervision—of the department manager.

The trend today is to wider spans and flatter structures, as shown in Figure 3.1. As we move away from command and control styles of leadership, managers can lead larger numbers. Thus the hierarchy becomes flatter. Fewer people are needed to supervise others. The flatter hierarchies lead to faster decisions, leaders who are in touch with organizational members, and lower overhead costs. But what is the best number in order for leaders to be able to provide help and training and make judgments about the work?

The Conference Board, a group that conducts research on organizational structures, recently conducted a survey of spans of supervision among its members. With thousands of observations from work groups, the distribution ranged from 0 to 127 people. The distribution was trimodal, with modes at 7, 17, and 75. (The *mode*—as distinguished from *mean* and *median* as descriptors of central tendency—is the value that occurs most frequently. In this case, three numbers frequently occurred; hence, there was a trimodal distribution.) How could this happen?

The traditional organizational model typically used spans of about seven people (and, apparently, a number of companies still do). To communicate with subordinates and evaluate them, managers had the time for only about seven people. The traditional span can be increased or decreased based on several factors.

FIGURE 3.1. Trends in Organizational Shapes.

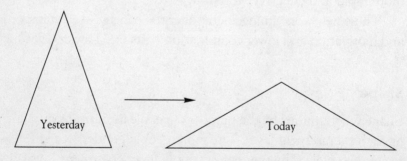

- The leader and group members are all experienced (so less communication and coaching are needed).
- Employees all do the same work.
- Each employee's task is independent of the others.
- The task is easily measured.

Thus, groups of salespeople may include fifteen to twenty people while software design groups may consist of only five.

Delegation of work by the leader to the group also results in wider spans. Indeed, some organizations widen spans to encourage more delegation. Some organizations today monitor spans in organizational units and set goals to widen them progressively. They train their managers to adopt more of a coaching style and less of a controlling style. So spans of about seventeen are very possible.

A different kind of organization is needed for spans of seventy-five people. An example is a factory with a plant manager and seventy-five blue-collar workers. The workers are organized into three teams of twenty-five people, with a team for each of the three shifts. Each team is self-managing. It selects, trains, disciplines, and rewards all its own members. The teams schedule the work and propose capital investments. The plant manager advises the teams and spends most time communicating with people outside the plant. Thus, the more the managerial work is delegated to work teams, the less the need for direct supervision. These kinds of teams lead to the elimination of levels of supervision and the complete elimination of command and control styles.

In sum, it is quite possible to observe companies following the traditional management model, choosing spans of about seven. More delegation and goal setting can lead to spans of around seventeen. For companies with policies of self-managing teams, spans of around seventy-five are possible. It is important to follow all the policies on the star model to create these teams (see Lawler, 1992).

When looking at the shape of an organization with the purpose of creating a flatter structure, the spans of supervision, rather than hierarchical levels, are examined. This is because spans are more easily analyzed and changed; it is harder to eliminate levels. The redundant level may be different in different departments: the first level may be easiest to eliminate in one function, the third level easiest in another. Span analysis would lead to a reduction of levels and would account for differences among departments. So when reducing levels, an approach that widens spans is easier to implement than one that focuses on levels.

Distribution of Power

Distribution of power in an organization refers to two concepts. The first is the vertical distribution of decision-making power and authority. This is called centralization or decentralization. Today, the trend is largely toward decentralizion of decision-making power, pushing the power down to people with direct product or customer contact.

The second concept is the horizontal distribution of power. The leader needs to shift power to the department dealing with mission-critical issues. Today in many competitive industries, the power to influence prices, terms, and conditions is shifting to the knowledgeable customer. So inside the organization, the decision-making power is shifting to units with direct customer contact. In industries where contracting out has raised purchased goods and services to 80 percent of cost of goods sold, the purchasing function is being given increased decision-making power. A task of the leader is to weigh continuously the business situation and tilt the balance of power when change is required.

Departmentalization

The activities of organizations involving more than two dozen people are grouped together to form departments. Departmentalization refers to the choice of departments to integrate the specialized work and form a hierarchy of departments. The choice of type of department is made at each hierarchical level. Departments are usually formed to include people working in one of the following areas:

1. A function or specialty
2. A product line
3. A customer segment
4. A geographical area
5. A work flow process

Each department type is appropriate for certain situations. The strategy and the size of the organization determines the choice.

Functional Structures. Most companies start by organizing around activities or functions. Companies of modest size usually adopt the functional structure shown in Figure 3.2. The diagram shows a typical Hewlett-Packard division.

The functional organization provides several advantages. First, gathering together all workers of one type—the R&D people, for example—allows them to transfer ideas, knowledge, and contacts among one other. Second, it allows them to achieve a greater level of specialization. When two hundred or so engineers are pooled, they can afford to dedicate some to such specialties as circuit designers

FIGURE 3.2. Functional Organization Structure.

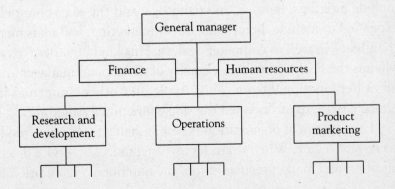

for gallium arsenide semiconductors. Third, using the example of a single purchasing function in operations, pooling the workers allows the company to present a single face to vendors and exercise buying leverage. Fourth, taking the example of using one manufacturing function to perform all production work, the company can afford to buy an expensive piece of test equipment and share it across product lines. Thus, the functional structure permits more scale and specialization than other structural alternatives for companies of a certain size.

Organizations with functional departments also promote standardization and reduce duplication. An activity that is organized functionally is performed in the same way and (presumably) in the best way throughout the company. The functions adopt one system or one policy for everyone rather than have each department invent its own. The functions adopt a single computer system, inventory control policy, absenteeism policy, and so on. Companies often revert back to the functional structure to reduce the proliferation and duplication of systems, standards, and policies that result from independent units not sharing or cooperating.

The functional organization has two weaknesses that frequently lead to the adoption of alternative structures. The first becomes apparent if a company offers a variety of products, services, channels, and customers. The situation is illustrated in Figure 3.3. Apple Computer used the functional organization to great advantage when it produced only Macintosh computers and sold them through computer dealers. However, the product line expanded to include desktops, laptops, and palmtops, and the sales channels expanded to include direct sales, direct marketing, and mass merchandisers, as well as computer dealers. This kind of variety overwhelms the decision-making capacity of the general manager and his or her functional team. Thus Apple, like other companies in similar situations, abandoned the single functional structure.

The functional organization is best at managing a single product or service line. When strategies involve product or service diversification and market segmentation, the functional organization is

FIGURE 3.3. Apple Before and After Reorganization.

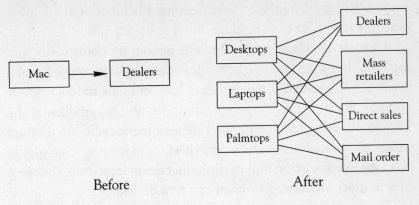

Before   After

either changed by organizing departments around products and markets or enhanced by the lateral processes. (The latter are described in Chapters Four and Five.)

The other weakness of the functional structure is the barrier created between different functions, inhibiting cross-functional processes such as new product development. When a company has only one product line (that does not change often) and when long product development cycles are feasible, the functional organization can manage the cross-functional processes and simultaneously deliver scale, expertise, and efficiency. But mass customization, short product life cycles, and rapid product development times overwhelm the functional structure. Thus today this structure is being replaced by product, market, or process structures and by lateral cross-functional processes.

Thus, the functional organization is appropriate for small companies and for those that need proprietary expertise and scale. It is appropriate if product and market variety is small, and if product life and development cycles are long. It is declining in popularity because in many industries, speed is more important than scale, and responsiveness to variety from any source is a condition for survival.

Product Structures. The functional structure is usually superseded by a product structure. When a company diversifies its product lines and those lines achieve minimum efficient scale for their own manufacturing, the company creates multiple functional organizations, each with its own product line (see Figure 3.4).

Hewlett-Packard and 3M became famous for continually subdividing divisions and product lines when scale permitted. Each division focused on a single product line and new product development. Forming departments or divisions around products is the best way to compress the product development cycle. So product structures became the standard method for managing strategies of product diversification and new product development. To create a new product, management created a new division.

But product structures have their own weaknesses. Product general managers all want autonomy. Each product division then reinvents the wheel, duplicating resources and generally missing opportunities for sharing. These features are the strengths of the functional structure. Therefore, companies usually augment the product structures with lateral functional processes, as we will see in Chapters Four and Five.

Another weakness of product structures is the possible loss of economies of scale. Not all functions can be divided into product units without a scale loss. These functions are often kept centralized

FIGURE 3.4. Product Structure.

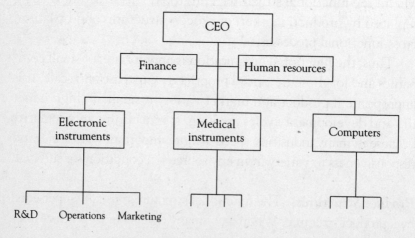

and shared. This situation creates hybrid structures that are mostly product but have a central shared function.

At Boeing's commercial aircraft group, the design and manufacture of planes is divided into product lines of narrow bodies (737, 757) and wide bodies (747, 767, and eventually the 777). However, the fabrication of major structural components requires very large and expensive computer-controlled machine tools. These would be too expensive to duplicate in each product line. Instead, a central fabrication unit is created and all manufacturing activities requiring scale and skill are placed in it and shared across product lines. The structure, shown in Figure 3.5, is a hybrid of products and functions. A similar situation can occur with the purchasing function. Today many companies are contracting out their component manufacturing. Purchased material can become as much as 80 percent of the cost of goods sold. A central purchasing or procurement function can become a central shared function.

The biggest challenge to the product structure comes from customers who buy from more than one product division. In the past, a central sales function was created to handle all products. But today customers want sourcing relationships, information exchange, electronic data interchange, single point of contact, and one invoice. These demands are forcing companies to create customer or market segment structures as a front end of the business to

FIGURE 3.5. Hybrid Product and Function Structure.

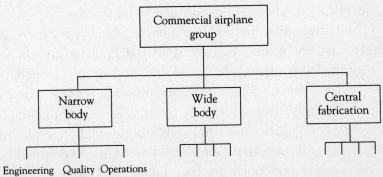

complement a product-focused back end. (The front/back model will be discussed in Chapter Seven.)

In summary, the product structure was, and in some cases still is, the organizational structure of choice for manufacturing companies, allowing them to manage strategies of product diversification and rapid development. The negative features of this structure may be compensated for by functional lateral processes, by central functions, and, increasingly, by the front/back model.

Market Structures

The most rapidly increasing type of structure is the one based on customers, markets, or industries. There are several reasons for the popularity.

The first reason is the shift in power in many industries to the buyer. Increased global competition has created more capacity than demand in many industries, thereby giving the buyer more choices. The buyer is aware of the choice and is learning how to use this new-found buying power. In many cases, buyers are insisting on dedicated units to serve their needs.

Second, the decline of scale in manufacturing—combined with higher-volume, single-sourcing arrangements—makes it economical for a supplier to dedicate a unit to serve a customer. For example, 7-Eleven of Japan has chosen Ajinomoto as the sole supplier of some food products and given it a large volume of business. Ajinomoto, in return, has created a unit to manufacture and sell products exclusively to 7-Eleven stores in Japan.

Third, the shift to market structures is enabled by the increased trend toward and willingness to contract out. Previously, a function that required scale might have forced the company into a functional or hybrid structure. Today, if the scale function is not a source of competitive advantage, it can be contracted out. For example, recording companies can form labels around small, fast-moving market segment units that perform all functions and contract out the essential but not critical compact disc manufacturing. (Actually, contracting out could enable any of the nonfunctional structures to be adopted.)

Fourth, there is a shift of competitive advantage to those companies with superior knowledge and information about market segments. Inexpensive information technology, access to databases and networks, bar code data, and so on, allow a company organized by market segment to gain superior knowledge about the preferences, buying habits, and lifestyles of customers in those segments. It can then create products and services that offer superior value to those customers. In the music business, a company usually organizes around market segments—classical, rock, country, rap, and so on. Recording companies create a label for each segment. The segment focuses on its customers and artists. The winners are the ones that attract the top talent and know the customers best.

The final reason for the increased popularity of the customer structure is the increasing proportion of service businesses in operation today. Service businesses usually focus on—and organize around—market segments. Services are usually customized and personalized for various segments of the population or industry. Banks, telecommunications firms like MCI, hotels like Marriott, and engineering and construction firms focus on market segments and industries for their divisions.

Market structures have negatives that are similar to those of product structures. Market divisions have a tendency to duplicate activities and develop incompatible systems. They may reduce scale if there is no contracting out. (Hybrid structures that centralize and share purchasing or central telecom networks at regional Bell companies can achieve market focus and efficient scale simultaneously.) They also have difficulty sharing common products or services, which may go to several market segments. Banks may provide a cash management service to customer segments based on their size, such as multinational firms, large corporations, and medium-size companies. Banks would like the segments to share the expensive cash management system bought by all segments and not duplicate it in each market unit.

Thus, organizations structured upon market or customer divisions are the fastest-growing kind. Their popularity reflects their compatibility with increasing buyer power, sourcing arrangements, declining scale, contracting out, the shift to the service economy, and especially the increasing competitive advantage of superior market segment knowledge and information.

Geographical Structures. Geographical structures traditionally developed as companies expanded their offerings across territories. There was usually a need to be close to the customer and to minimize the costs of travel and distribution. Sometimes industries, like timber and coal, needed to locate near sources of supply. Today, the economics of location is important but information technology is making it less important in certain industries. The use of geographical structure depends entirely on the industry.

In service industries where the service is provided on-site, geography continues to be a structural basis for many companies. Service businesses and sales and service functions have always been geographically organized around districts, regions, and areas. McDonald's and Pizza Hut have geographical structures; the regions are influenced by span of control choices and the economics of distribution of food ingredients. Foodservice companies are likely to have flatter structures in the future, but they will still be geographical.

Geography is becoming less important in other sales and service activities. Sales forces and knowledge services—like consulting—were traditionally managed out of local offices, based on personal relationships and knowledge of the region. Relationships are still important, but industry knowledge and expertise are becoming more important: to sell to banks, one must be well-versed in the banking industry. As a result, industry or market segment structures are being adopted. Sales are also being made through electronic markets, direct computer access by a customer, 800 numbers, and catalogues. Selling today requires fewer office calls by expensive direct sales forces.

However, changes to the geographical structure are occurring in industries where the technology is creating smaller efficient scale and flexible plants and where customers demand just-in-time delivery. Functional organizations are being replaced by multiple, small, fast profit centers. Smaller factories can be located close to the customer and produce a variety of products to service all the needs of their customers. For example, Frito-Lay moved to a geographical structure recently. The company capitalizes on information captured by bar code scanners to move product with limited shelf life rapidly and frequently, and to move quickly on promotions.

The role of geography in manufacturing is complex, with a relationship between the ratio of product value to transport cost, and attention to the minimum efficient scale of a factory. Cement and paper are low-cost commodities with high transport costs. Such companies use regional profit centers. In contrast, semiconductors and pharmaceuticals are high-value items with low transport costs. They are global products and geography is less important and product more important in determining the organizational structures of these firms.

Service companies that provide information and knowledge processing are increasingly becoming location-free. The engineering and construction industries can gain an edge with effective geographical structure. At an oil company's new Asian refinery, the initial high-skilled work is performed at the company's North American offices, where their leading design skills are located. Most of this work is located in Los Angeles, but the Calgary and Houston offices have excess capacity and need work. Thus, some design activities are moved electronically to these offices and coordinated through a common computer system. At the completion of the high-level design, the work is beamed over satellite to a group of three hundred Filipino engineers. They generate the fifteen thousand drawings to guide the construction work. This lower-skilled work is more cost effective when performed in the Philippines at Filipino wages.

Companies are seeking the best global location because they can be moved anywhere. Insurance companies send claims forms overnight to Ireland to be processed and returned by satellite the next day. With the new information technology, much service work can be moved anywhere in this way, creating the location-free organization.

Many other service activities are becoming location-free. The elevator business was one in which companies made their money on the service contract and spare parts. A worldwide, geographically structured service organization was a competitive advantage. However, things have changed; today, elevators are designed not to fail. Electronic components mean fewer moving parts and less need for timely, nearby service calls. There is also a large component of software in elevator controls, which can be monitored and repaired from any remote location. Sensors can be installed in critical areas of potential failure. When monitors at a remote location report a likely failure, repair crews can be dispatched from their bases. The monitoring and repair crews can be located in the most cost-effective areas of the world, provided those locations have skilled people and good telecom and airport infrastructures.

Process Structures. The newest organizational structure is the process structure. There is considerable variation in what people are calling a process organization, however. In general, a process structure is based on a complete flow of work, such as that of the order fulfillment process. This process flows from initiation by a customer order, through the functions, to delivery to the customer. Currently, each function performs a part of the work along the sequential flow. The advocates of the process organization—sometimes also called the horizontal organization—suggest that the people from each function who work on the process should be gathered into a process team and given end-to-end responsibility for the overall process. The process team reports to a process leader. The structure is thereby converted from a vertical functional structure to a horizontal process structure, as shown in Figure 3.6.

FIGURE 3.6. Process Organization Structure.

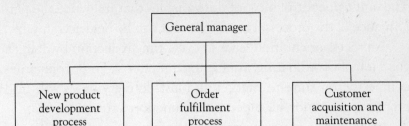

The process structure is the culmination of three strategic initiatives that all focused on work flow processes and fought against the barriers of the functional structure. The first was total quality (TQ). TQ efforts all promote understanding processes, controlling processes, and improving processes in order to meet criteria defined by the customer. Cross-functional coordination is essential. The second initiative was cycle-time reduction. The attainment of speed requires tight coordination across functions. Finally, reengineering brought the new information technology to bear on the redesign of the processes themselves. Clearly, the momentum for a process orientation has been building for some time.

The process structure has been offered as an alternative to the functional structure. And there is much to recommend it. Perhaps the greatest benefit is a fresh look, from end to end, at the whole process. When combined with new information technologies, there is considerable opportunity for redesign of an entire process. A change in one function's piece may make an enormous difference in the pieces of the other functions. By having one manager in charge of the whole process rather than individual managers for each function, the resistance to process change can be overcome.

A process with end-to-end coverage also lends itself to measurement more easily than functions do. Each function is responsible for a piece of the process. A unit responsible for the entire process is responsible for a reasonably self-contained piece of work. The unit can control most of the variables that influence the performance of the process. Hence, the unit can be held accountable.

A process orientation leads to cycle-time reduction by doing a good job of coordinating work across functions. Thus, companies competing on time-to-market and fast-delivery bases will find process organization far superior to a functional structure.

In addition, some costs are reduced with a process organization. The faster time cycles mean reduced inventories and faster receipt of cash. The reduced working capital translates into reduced costs of carrying inventory and cash. Other costs are reduced because duplication of work across functions is eliminated. With a functional structure, often one division will not trust the input of another and will check and rework information to its own satisfaction. A process organization eliminates such redundant activities, verifying input once for all functions.

The process organization is therefore superior to the functional organization in businesses with short product life and development cycles. It is also superior when the redesign of processes has great potential for reducing costs and satisfying the customer. In contrast, the functional organization is superior for companies with long cycles and where scale and expertise are important. Yet the benefits of a process orientation can still be obtained by creating lateral process teams, which coordinate across the functional structure.

When compared with the functional organization, the process organization can break down barriers and achieve significant savings. However, the structure should be adopted with care. It is currently fashionable, which means the weaknesses associated with it get suppressed. When compared with product or market segment structures, it is not yet clear how the process structure stacks up. Product and market structures have themselves knocked down functional barriers and achieved end-to-end focus on products and customers. And the process structure creates its own barriers—for example, a handoff between the new product process group and the order fulfillment process group, as a product moves from new to existing status. In contrast, the product organization would be seamless on this issue.

Ultimately, combining a process focus within a product or market structure should prove to be a powerful productivity enhancer. It is probable that product, market, or geographical divisions will be the basic profit centers. The subunits within these profit centers will be divided into functions or processes that are useful within product or customer structures.

Choosing Structures

The leader's first organizational design choice is the basic structure. This choice process begins with an understanding of the business's strategy. By matching what is required by the strategy to what is done best by the various structures, a decision can be made. The kinds of strategies executed best by the basic structures are listed as follows:

Functional Structure

- Small-size, single-product line
- Undifferentiated market
- Scale or expertise within the function
- Long product development and life cycles
- Common standards

Product Structure

- Product focus
- Multiple products for separate customers
- Short product development and life cycle
- Minimum efficient scale for functions or outsourcing

Market Structure

- Important market segments
- Product or service unique to segment
- Buyer strength
- Customer knowledge advantage
- Rapid customer service and product cycles
- Minimum efficient scale in functions or outsourcing

Geographical Structure

- Low value-to-transport cost ratio
- Service delivery on-site
- Closeness to customer for delivery or support
- Perception of the organization as local
- Geographical market segments needed

Process Structure

- Best seen as an alternative to the functional structure
- Potential for new processes and radical change to processes
- Reduced working capital
- Need for reducing process cycle times

Unfortunately, in the typical situation no one type of structure best fits the business strategy. The decision maker should list the strengths and weaknesses of each structural alternative. The decision maker must also develop priorities for strategic attributes, such as cycle-time reduction or scale of manufacturing. Then the choice of structure can be made for the top priorities. The structural alternatives that are runners-up become candidates for hybrid structures or for lateral coordination processes.

This chapter discussed the concept of structure in general and departmental structures in particular. Although the traditional hierarchy is losing favor, flatter hierarchies will be with us for some time. The functional, product, market, geographical, and process alternatives were all analyzed and their strengths and weaknesses identified. For some structures, the weaknesses can be overcome with hybrid structures. For others, lateral processes can augment the basic structures. Indeed, to be responsive on multiple dimensions, lateral processes are key. These processes will be discussed in the next two chapters.

4

Linking Processes to Coordination Needs

Most of the activity in an organization does not follow the vertical hierarchical structure. As continuous change becomes the natural state in most industries, lateral processes become the principal means of coordinating activities.

Lateral processes are information and decision processes that coordinate activities spread out across different organizational units. Lateral processes are mechanisms for decentralizing general management decisions. They accomplish the decentralization by recreating the organization in microcosm for the issue at hand. That is, each department with information about—and a stake in—an issue contributes a representative for issue resolution, as shown in Figure 4.1.

No matter what type of hierarchical structure is chosen, some activities will require coordination across departments. Most organizations deal with a complex world. They have to do business with multiple customers, multiple partners, multiple suppliers. They have to compete with rivals in many areas of the world. They deal with governments, regulators, distributors, labor unions, and trade associations. They employ different skill specialties, using multiple technologies while producing a variety of products and services. If a company creates an organization to maximize its effectiveness in

FIGURE 4.1. Lateral Processes Across Departments.

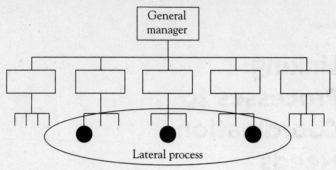

Source: Galbraith, 1994, p. 6.

dealing with one constituency—for example, customers—it fragments its ability to deal with others—for example, unions. All the dimensions not handled by the structure require coordination through lateral management processes.

Today, these other dimensions are increasing in number and importance. In addition to focusing on more powerful and knowledgeable customers, a company must leverage its own buying power, concentrate its R&D investments on its leading technologies and core competencies, and become a good citizen in regions where active host governments negotiate relationships. Companies must focus simultaneously on governments, customers, functions, vendors, and products. Lateral processes are designed to provide the company with the capability of addressing all of these concerns. Today a company must create a multidimensional organization built around its basic structure. A company must be flexible in addressing whatever unpredictable issue arises, whether it presents a threat or an opportunity.

Lateral Coordination

The organization designer must match the amount of lateral coordination needed to execute a multidimensional strategy with different types and amounts of lateral processes. To learn how to match coordination needs and lateral processes, let us examine a single-business, functional structure, and its cross-functional lateral processes. (The functional structure is the most common organizational structure. For more on this, see Chapter Three of this volume. For a discussion of lateral processes across subsidiaries and business units, see Galbraith, 1994.)

The management challenge for a functional organization is to coordinate the cross-functional work flows, as indicated in Figure 4.2. Coordination across functions—to create and deliver products or services—is the responsibility of the general manager and his or her management team. As mentioned in Chapter Three, this coordination is most easily accomplished when the company produces a single line of products or services for a single customer type, and when product life and development cycles are long.

But the need for lateral coordination will exceed the capacity of the team at the top when a company's strategies and tasks involve the following:

- Diversity
- Rapid change
- Interdependence of units

FIGURE 4.2 Work Flows Across Functional Structure.

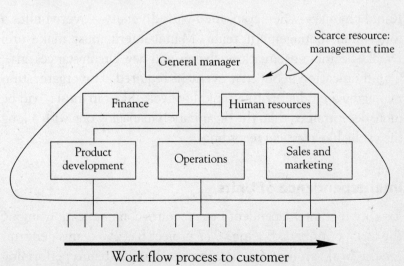

- A process focus
- Speed

To deal with these forces, management may have to change the entire structure of an organization. But another alternative is to enlist lateral processes, which may be thought of as "general manager equivalents." These processes offer a different, more subtle approach to decentralizing decisions and increasing decision-making capacity. The types and amounts of lateral processes used will vary depending on the relative importance of the five forces.

Diversity

The more variety in a company's work, the more decentralization is needed. No functional management team can handle the priority setting required by multiple products in multiple markets. For example, Apple has evolved from a company offering a single product sold through dealers in the United States to one offering many products sold through multiple channels domestically as well as in Europe, Asia, and Latin America.

Rapid Change

Rapid change—when combined with diversity—overwhelms a functional management team. Management must make and remake decisions as situations change and new circumstances arise. Communication about new events is required. The organization managing a product with a rapid life cycle, like rap music, will be more decentralized than the organization managing one with a long life cycle, like classical recordings.

Interdependence of Units

Execution of interdependent tasks requires communication among the task performers. Boeing's 777 project has 250 teams performing the work; an investment bank also has 250 teams performing its work. Boeing's teams are design-and-build teams for sections of the aircraft, such as the wing, the cockpit, and the avionics. These teams are tightly integrated and communicate frequently. In contrast, the investment bank's teams work on 250 separate deals for separate clients. Each team can act independently because its work will not affect the others. These teams are less interdependent. They require less coordination than the Boeing teams do.

A Process Focus

Process-focused efforts, like total quality management and reengineering, examine work flows across functions and aim at continuously improving processes. A process focus leads to more cross-functional coordination and inevitably to lateral management processes.

Speed

Finally, cycle-time reduction demands for new products, customer orders, and customer service requests substantially increase the need for cross-functional coordination. To accomplish these reductions, decisions must be moved to the points of product and customer contact; there simply is no time to go up the hierarchy to find a general manager. Lateral processes create a general manager equivalent at the point of action.

Thus, collectively these five forces determine the need for cross-functional coordination and the correlating amount of cross-functional lateral processes. It is important to recognize that the need varies, from low (for companies manufacturing beer or producing classical music titles, for example) to high (for those producing multimedia products and rap music titles).

The Benefits and Costs of Lateral Processes

As noted, the task of the organization designer is to match the type and amount of lateral processes with the cross-functional coordination required by the firm's business strategy. The designer must avoid choosing too little or too many lateral processes. Up to a point, lateral processes produce benefits; thereafter, they increase costs and difficulty.

What are the benefits of lateral processes? The benefits involve permitting the company to make more decisions, different kinds of decisions, and better and faster decisions.

Because lateral processes decentralize general management decisions, they free up top management for other decisions. Thus they increase the capacity of the organization to make more decisions more often. The organization is therefore more adaptable to constant change. Different types of decisions are made and can address the multiple dimensions of a business environment. Companies decentralize choice to the points of product and customer contact where decisions can be made and implemented quickly because these groups may have access to current and local information available only to them.

A business may have a functional structure but, by enlisting lateral processes, it becomes capable of forming new product teams, customer teams, and process teams for reengineering. The business is therefore flexible, no matter the issue at hand.

However, lateral processes can also create costs. The decentralized decisions may not be better than those of top management. The people may not have the perspective and experience of top management. These costs can be minimized, however, by making the organization's total data base available, by training people, and providing the correct incentives.

Another cost comes in the form of the time of the people involved. With today's flat and lean hierarchical structures, employee time is at a premium. Time spent on a reengineering team is time not spent with customers or developing new hires. The more time spent on teams, the greater the cost. Lateral processes can be seen as investments of management time to create shorter cycle times.

The third cost comes in increased level of conflict. Cross-functional teams are made up of representatives who see issues differently. Much of the time involved in cross-functional processes is devoted to communicating, problem solving, and resolving conflicts. The company that is skilled at conflict resolution can lower the costs and time needed to reach decisions.

Thus, there are both benefits and costs to lateral processes. The designer needs to find the point of balance. This balance can be struck by matching coordination needs with the different types and amounts of lateral processes.

The Three Types of Lateral Processes

There are three basic types of lateral processes, as shown in Figure 4.3. They vary in the amount of management time and energy that must be invested in them.

Informal or voluntary lateral processes occur spontaneously. They are the least expensive and easiest form to use. Although they occur naturally, organization designers can greatly improve the frequency and effectiveness of these voluntary processes.

The next type of lateral process, which requires more time commitment, is formal groups. Teams or task forces are formally created,

FIGURE 4.3. Types of Lateral Processes.

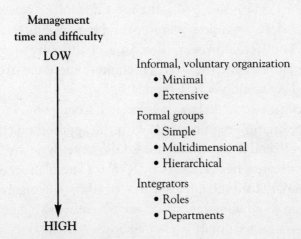

Management
time and difficulty

LOW

Informal, voluntary organization
- Minimal
- Extensive

Formal groups
- Simple
- Multidimensional
- Hierarchical

Integrators
- Roles
- Departments

HIGH

Source: Galbraith, 1994, p. 36.

members appointed, charters defined, and goals set for the cross-functional effort. Formal groups are more costly than voluntary groups because they are the creation of management and do not occur naturally. They require some team building and maintenance for proper functioning.

Formal groups are also more costly because they are used in addition to the voluntary groups, not instead of them. The organization needs both voluntary efforts and formal groups to supplement the general manager's coordination across functions. The simpler forms are still needed but are insufficient by themselves to achieve the integration the strategy requires.

The third level of commitment to lateral processes comes with appointment of integrators to lead the formal groups. At some point, full-time leaders may be required. Leaders may be product managers, project managers, process managers, brand managers, and so on. They are all "little general managers," who manage a product or service in place of the general manger. They are enlisted because there are many products, new products, and rapid life cycles.

Using integrators is the most costly lateral process. In addition to the cumulative costs of the voluntary processes and the formal groups that must already be in place, using integrators requires hiring a group of full-time people whose task is to integrate the efforts of others. The integrator role is also the most difficult to execute. Integrators introduce confusion over roles and responsibilities and an element of conflict. However, the cost and difficulty may be judged appropriate because the strategy requires functional excellence and rapid generation of new products or services.

Thus, the organization designer must match a company's cross-functional coordination requirements with the appropriate types and amounts of lateral processes. Figure 4.4 illustrates how the five strategic forces create a need for varying levels of lateral processes.

The remainder of this chapter will describe how the organization designer can foster voluntary processes. The other two types of lateral processes—formal groups and integrators—will be discussed in depth in the next chapter.

FIGURE 4.4. Matching Coordination Needs with Lateral Processes.

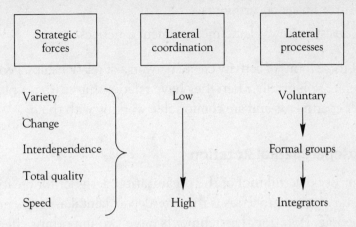

Fostering Voluntary Processes

An organization characterized by voluntary coordination across units is usually referred to as an informal organization. The process seems to occur naturally and spontaneously. For example, a discussion between a salesperson and a customer leads to an idea for a product change. The salesperson and an engineer make a preliminary design. The design is sent to operations and marketing for their ideas. A new product results a few weeks later, all because of the voluntary cooperation of people in different units.

Such acts may occur hundreds of times each day and can be a source of great strength for the company. But great weakness occurs when the voluntary acts do not happen. In many cases these acts do not occur because of cross-functional barriers.

Today there is great interest in removing barriers and encouraging voluntary cooperation. Leaders can employ a number of actions to elicit voluntary cooperation:

1. Interdepartmental rotation
2. Interdepartmental events
3. Colocation

4. Information technology
5. Mirror image departments
6. Consistent reward and measurement practices

All of these forms of activity create networks of relationships. People cooperate voluntarily when they have relationships with people in other departments and are comfortable working with them.

Interdepartmental Rotation

The most powerful tool of the organization designer for creating voluntary lateral processes is the interdepartmental assignment of key people. Rotational assignments have two important effects. First, they train and develop people in all facets of the business. People who are successful at rotational assignments learn how to learn, they do not simply gain the specific knowledge of the business. The rotated managers can more effectively participate in cross-functional teams. They can chair the teams and grow into integrators. Rotations create generalists and the general management capability that is at the heart of lateral processes. Individuals become more flexible and if we are to create flexible organizations, we need flexible people. These people also develop relationships in the various departments. These relationships then can be used later in lateral coordination attempts.

Thus, rotational assignments create a lateral communication network across the company (see Galbraith, 1994, pp. 46–50). Taken together, the trained individuals and the relationships they have cultivated create the organizational capability for lateral coordination. Rotational experiences simultaneously develop the individual and build his or her relationships, thereby developing the voluntary organization. The task of the organization designer is to make sure that relationships are created at key work flow interfaces where coordination is required.

However, rotations also create costs. People are less effective when they are learning new roles. When managers are reluctant to give up good people and train newcomers, effort and time from the leader is needed to keep the rotation process in motion. But the cost of rotations, which should realistically be considered an "investment" instead of a "cost" as it develops individuals, creates a network of relationships, and builds a flexible, lateral capability.

Interdepartmental Events

Voluntary processes also result from events, such as training courses and conferences. Indeed, training budgets are as justified by their networking effects as by their developmental effects. The organization designer only needs to decide who should attend. Also, like rotational assignments, events are most effective when they create relationships across the key work flow interfaces.

Colocation

Proximity of employees is an important factor in fostering productive relationships. There is good evidence that reducing distance and physical barriers between people increases the amount of communication between them. Engineering firms colocate everyone working on a project. As projects come and go, the firms reconfigure the organization and the office layouts.

The organization designer needs to give careful thought to location patterns. For example, if a marketing group is located close to an operations group perhaps it is not located close to engineering. Once again, the designer needs to know the key interfaces where communication is most necessary and relationships most likely to be productive.

Information Technology Networks

Another powerful method used to create lateral processes is the new information technology. Within a few years, it will be possible for any employee to communicate with anyone else in the organization. It is important that organization designers participate in the creation of the architectures and software underlying this powerful organization shaper.

Global consulting firms are probably the most advanced in this area. A consultant can call upon a database to see who is currently working on—or who has recently completed—an assignment involving the organization of regional banks. Individuals can easily create their own networks to exchange information and expertise through electronic bulletin boards.

Organization designers can also create links through the use of software, such as Lotus Notes™. All people working with Citibank or Sony, for example, can be linked in a network to exchange information. A database of facts and figures can be created to support questions commonly asked about Citibank. Organization designers can create these electronic networks or teams across the structure. (These teams are currently referred to as "virtual teams"; that is, they are not real teams but are linked electronically to behave as if they were.)

It is important to recognize that technology alone cannot create the lateral processes. Technology creates the connections between people. But connection does not necessarily lead to communication. Technology leads to more communication within interpersonal networks where people have some affinity for one another and share a common language. When people already have the relationships, then technology is a great facilitator. When people have common goals and purposes, the communication can lead to coordination.

As suggested in Figure 4.5, it takes an organization designed to use information technology to create useful lateral coordination processes.

Mirror Image Departments

One of the greatest barriers to lateral processes is the sheer number of interfaces across which people must communicate to gain a consensus for action. Usually, each function organizes according to its

FIGURE 4.5. Technology Networks to Coordination.

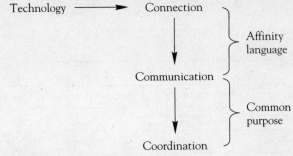

Source: Galbraith, 1994, p. 59.

own logic. For example, in a consumer packaged goods company, over twenty interfaces would have to be worked for a salesperson and an engineer to modify a product. Sales is organized by geography, marketing by brands, manufacturing by site and process, engineering by product, purchasing by commodity and vendor. It would take an engineer an unrealistic amount of time to communicate with and gain support from each function.

In response, some companies have organized their functions as mirror images of one another. Figure 4.6 shows how an airplane manufacturer has organized each function around major sections of the aircraft. A manager of the wing, for example, has an interface in each other function. Each person has to work five or six interfaces in order to get complete support. These five or six people can form the equivalent of a general manager for the wing, tail, avionics, and so on. Decisions can be decentralized to these groups, with each group assuming end-to-end responsibility for their section of the aircraft. It is an easy next step to formalize the group and have it set group goals for cycle time, quality, and cost improvements.

The mirror image structure creates a clear line of sight across the entire organization. It can facilitate establishment of relationships by simplifying the interfaces across which lateral processes take place. The managers get to know one another and spend less communication time getting an end-to-end commitment to a decision. The likelihood of voluntary cooperation is much higher.

FIGURE 4.6. Mirror Image Functional Structure.

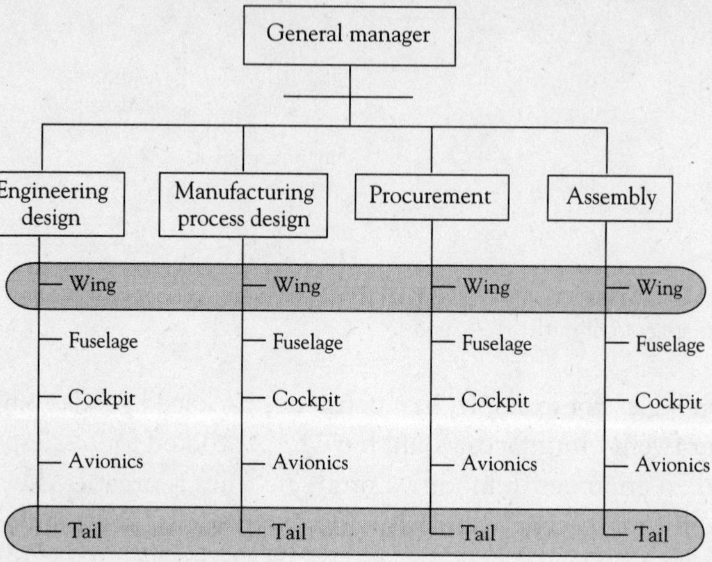

Source: Galbraith, 1994, p. 57.

However, there is a cost to this structure. It is tantamount to organizing by product or process at the level below the functional manager. It creates the costs that are associated with those structures, such as loss of scale, duplication, and so on. Often, the costs are accepted in order to get the coordination and cycle-time reduction. Or the designer can create a hybrid structure within the function.

Consistent Reward and Measurement Systems

One of the keys to creating voluntary processes across units is to align the interests of the parties involved. Often, functional measurements designed independently of each other create incompatible goals, causing another barrier to cross-functional cooperation. A task of the leader is to test for cross-unit consistency of goals and to design supporting reward systems. Performance measurement and reward systems are useful tools for creating aligned goals and objectives. Often, a common goal, like cycle-time reduction, can apply across all functions. Or there may be a customer for the cross-functional work. The group can start with what the customer wants in order to generate measurement criteria. But in any case, clear consistent measures, goals, and correlated rewards are needed to promote voluntary cooperation across units.

Summary

The leader as organization designer can choose any or all of the methods described to foster the use of voluntary processes. The leader needs to become skilled at these methods, because more and more coordination processes are taking place at the grassroots level on a voluntary basis. The increasing availability of new information technology will continue the trend, as more decisions continue to be made at the point of customer contact by cross-functional groups.

As mentioned earlier in this chapter, a key goal of the organization designer is to match the coordination needs of the business's strategy with the appropriate types and amount of lateral processes. To implement simple business strategies, a functional structure and voluntary processes may be sufficient. But for many companies today, more coordination is needed to address all of the dimensions of the strategy. Formal groups and integrators may then be the solution. These are discussed in the next chapter.

5

Creating and Integrating Group Processes

The decision to augment voluntary lateral processes with formal processes—either formal groups or formal groups plus integrators—will make the leader more of a decision shaper. The voluntary processes, described in Chapter Four, arise spontaneously; they are a form of organization from the bottom up. With the formal lateral processes, the leader is more directly involved in the creation, the staffing, and the goal setting. Thus there is more organization from the top down.

There are several reasons for a more active role by the leader in the design of the lateral processes. If an issue arises and no voluntary process forms in response, management must create a group to deal with the issue. Management—from its perspective—may, in fact, become aware of an issue before it even appears to be an issue at the lower levels of the organization. Or management may want to augment or modify a voluntary process already in existence.

From a more global perspective, management shapes a lateral process to make it more compatible with other efforts, with resources, and with the overall strategy. For example, at the grassroots level an issue may be seen as a sales and marketing problem, while from management's viewpoint the issue may be larger, involving operations as well. Thus, management may want to increase or change membership in a cross-functional team. It may add a person who would profit from the experience or an experienced person who could commit more resources.

Finally, management must set priorities about the types and amount of lateral processes it wishes to undertake. With limited resources, a company cannot simultaneously undertake product, customer, process, vendor, and improvement teams. Management must set priorities about where talent needs to be invested. The priorities should set the strategic direction and focus the organization.

Formal Groups

Formal groups augment the efforts of voluntary processes. When there is a need for more decision making, a team, task force, or council is created to focus on a set of issues. However, rather than being a substitute for voluntary processes, formal groups are used in addition to them and, indeed, build on the same capabilities. There is currently a great deal of writing about using teams (Cohen, 1993; Smith and Katzenbach, 1992) and about team building (Dyer, 1988).

Design of Formal Groups

All groups, no matter what type, are subject to the same design choices. These are summarized as follows:

Bases. The bases of lateral processes are the same as the bases for structure, that is, function, product, market, geography, and work flow. If one is chosen for the structure, the other four are candidates for lateral processes. Each candidate has the same positives and negatives as the structural type. Just as strategy drives the choice of structure, it should help set the priorities here. The organization designer should also decide how much time and effort should be devoted to each.

Charter. The scope, mission, and authority of the groups must be defined. What issues are to be addressed? What resource levels can the group commit? Management should define the groups' charters so that they are compatible with the charter of the hierarchical structure and supplement it. In addition, management should look for overlapping efforts between various groups and define conflict resolution processes.

Staffing. The people who participate in a group are central to its efficient functioning. A representative should be chosen from each affected unit. All should have a position within their unit that gives them access to the information relevant to the issues that will be addressed and the authority to commit their unit. If the group is to be a unit making decisions in reasonable time frames, members must possess both information and authority. The roles created by mirror image structures are ideal for this purpose.

The mirror image structure also creates roles in which the manager's job in the vertical hierarchy is consistent with the job in the lateral processes. A less than ideal situation is when the managers of a company are spread across thirty to thirty-five teams. Each manager has four or five team assignments in addition to a full-time job. Very little will be accomplished in these teams. Organization designers should strive to staff groups so that managers are given only one cross-functional team assignment. Further, the team assignment should have as much overlap as possible with their full-time job.

Conflict. Conflict management is a required skill in an ever-changing world. The group needs an approach to manage constructively the inevitable differences in points of view. Individual members need group problem solving and conflict management skills. The purpose is to use different points of view to stimulate information exchange and learning. Although each member will see a portion of a situation, the group problem solving will afford a total view.

Rewards. Participants will have little energy with which to confront conflict and problem solving if they perceive little reward resulting from their efforts (Lawler, 1990). The person's team performance should count as much as the line job performance in evaluations. The team performance component can be gauged from the meeting of team goals, such as cycle time. Additional input can come from evaluations of other team members or of the team leader.

Leader Role. There is an emerging view that teams may not need a formal leader. And indeed, for groups with a reasonable number of members and some self-management experience, a designated leader may not be required. Instead, a different leader will emerge depending on the issue at hand and those in the group most capable to handle it. Most organizations, however, designate a leader to plan agendas, convene the group, lead discussions, and communicate the group's decisions.

Rather than creating a full-time integrator role, a leader may be chosen from the function most affected by the group task or from a dominant function. Boeing design-and-build teams are led by design engineers; Procter and Gamble brand teams are led by advertising brand managers. In both cases, the natural work closely resembles that of the leadership task.

Another option is a rotating leader. The leader changes as the function most affected changes with each successive stage of the group's work. For example, Dow-Corning rotates the leader of new product teams. Initially the leader comes from R&D, then from manufacturing, and eventually from marketing as the product nears distribution. Over the product development cycle, the group gets a general management leader, but gets it through sequential handoffs from one function to another.

Simple Group Structures

The design of lateral group structures can vary from simple ones, with a few cross-functional product teams, to complex multidimensional and multilevel structures. The coordination needs of the strategy will dictate how complex a form is necessary.

The use of simple teams has been a management strategy for some time, since the aerospace companies began using cross-functional teams in the 1960s. Today, companies are focusing on work flows and creating cross-functional work flow teams to gain speed and reengineer processes.

In all simple structures, the designer tries to create an end-to-end task, so that the team has a complete piece of work. In this manner, the team controls most of the factors that influence its performance outcomes. The team can then be independently measured on its performance and held accountable for it. Management can give considerable decision-making power to such a group.

In the electronics industry, new products are introduced annually and last only eighteen months. Companies use cross-functional teams dedicated to the product for the entire eighteen months. The team develops the product, introduces it, manages it, and takes it off the market; the more complete the task, the more control the team has. It is thus easier for the team to generate a plan and for management to delegate decision making to it. The team is measured on total profitability over the product's life cycle, making it easier to reward the members for the team's performance.

Complex Group Structures

Teams can become complex for two reasons. The first is the size of the teams. As companies focus on work flows and attempt to put decision-making authority at points of contact with the work itself, the number of departments involved can rise. At some point, it is necessary to divide the overall process into subprocesses. The subprocesses are semiautonomous, with cross-functional teams of twenty to twenty-five people taking responsibility for each of them. These subdivisions create a design problem: trying to link the subprocesses for overall coordination of the work flow. The design of the linkages leads to complex lateral groups.

Teams also become complex when the business has multiple dimensions. Although the Boeing 777 design-and-build teams are created around sections of the product, Boeing also forms customer teams for customers like United Airlines or All Nippon Airways. The difficulty arises because the design-and-build teams want every plane to be the same in order to reduce costs and cycle time while the customer teams want the planes to be different for each customer. Hence, there is a need for dialogue and conflict resolution. Thus, complex structures become necessary when teams are interdependent and possibly in conflict. With complex team structures, the organization designer must solve two problems. First, the designer must create processes to coordinate and communicate across teams. Second, the designer must create a process to resolve interteam conflicts. Two examples will serve to illustrate these concepts.

Work Flow Process Team. Computer companies have complex order fulfillment processes, with a large number of departments working on a customer's order from issuance to delivery. These companies create subprocesses—such as order entry, inbound logistics, and outbound logistics—to form the entire process. The order entry portion processes the customer's order, which may involve several products and software from outside vendors. There are credit checks and pricing decisions. Often, there are custom design features involving engineering. Inbound logistics takes the customer orders and places orders on vendors. This team manages the receipt of material, accounts payable, raw material, and some in-process inventory, up to final assembly. The outbound logistics team manages assembly, delivery, and installation of the system at the customer site. It manages finished goods inventory, billing, and accounts receivable. There is a team for each subprocess. Each team has the discretion to manage its portion of the work flow, redesign it, and continuously improve it, but decisions made by one team must be consistent with those made by others.

Figure 5.1 illustrates this process. The overall work flow is indicated in the figure by the arrows. The linkage is achieved as two to

FIGURE 5.1. Teams to Manage Order Fulfillment.

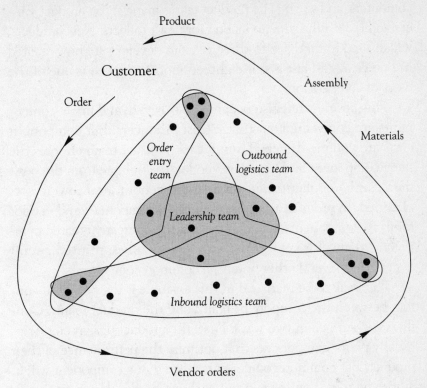

three members play liaison roles and participate in pairs of teams. The shaded areas show the engineers, manufacturing engineers, and purchasing managers who carry out the linking roles across teams. (The teams are linked, and form a hierarchy of teams—as opposed to a hierarchy of roles in a simple structure—to resolve conflict.) A leadership team is formed by the leaders of each team and an overall process leader. (This leader is an integrator; this role will be discussed in the next section of the chapter.) The leadership team sets decision criteria, communicates across teams, and quickly resolves conflicts.

Multidimensional Team. No less complex designs are needed for multidimensional team structures. A personal computer business is organized by function and uses cross-functional product teams for terminals, low-end personal computers, high-performance personal computers, and so on. The product teams manage the product variety and reduce the time to market for new products. New products, which used to take two to three years to develop, are now created in one year, and last about eighteen months. Speed is one of the bases of competition.

This business has also become cost-driven, and many components are contracted out to low-cost producers. But component costs are volume-driven. Thus, if each product team chooses the same component and the same vendor, the volume from the business can be concentrated on a single vendor, and lower costs obtained. In order to agree on a common component and vendor for each component on each product, the company created component teams for keyboards, cathode ray tubes, printed circuit boards, and several other potential common components.

The issue to be managed in this example is the potential conflict between the component teams and the product teams. Conflicts can surface in two ways. First, the product design engineers usually prefer components that optimize the performance of their product. But common components mean that a component will fit all products and optimize none of them. So the design engineers may fight the idea of using common components at all or they may disagree about which component should be the common one. The other point of conflict may involve the attempt to reach consensus across the product and component teams; this process can constrain the speed of the product design team. Top speed is attained when each team makes design decisions independently. The design of the team structure and the guidance from top management are the keys to achieving simultaneously common components and speedy launch of new products.

Top management of the computer company has articulated a strategy that places cost as the primary criterion for resolving conflicts. The strategy shifts the burden of proof to the engineers to show how a unique component will result in a substantial price and performance difference. Management also challenges the engineers to achieve high performance while using standard, common components. Top management's strategy is to provide criteria for decentralizing decisions to product and component teams. The same criteria serve the dispute settlement process across the teams.

The organizational design of the product teams and component teams is shown in Figure 5.2. Each product team is a cross-functional unit led by a product manager from engineering. Engineering and purchasing representatives working on printed circuit boards and keyboards are members of both the product teams and the component teams. They serve as the links between the two teams. They are joined on the component teams by their counterparts working on other product teams. Component teams are chaired by technically trained managers from purchasing. In turn, the component team leaders, product team leaders, and product managers all form a conflict resolution team chaired by the purchasing vice president. A manager from engineering, usually a computer architect, participates as well.

FIGURE 5.2. Product and Component Team Combination.

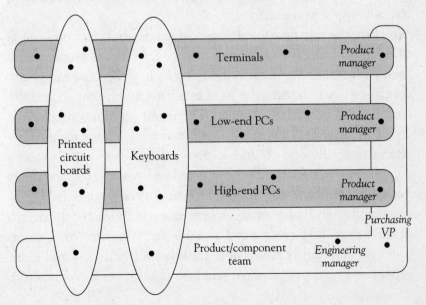

The key features of the design are the linkages. The engineering and purchasing representatives who participate on both teams are central to the coordination and communication between the teams. The other links are the people who serve as leaders of the two teams. Collectively, they constitute the conflict resolution team. They link the team efforts with a thorough but rapid appeal process.

In this example, the teams permit a functional organization to focus simultaneously on products and on component vendors. With purchased components accounting for 70 percent to 80 percent of cost of goods sold, and with product speed and cost central to the customer purchase decision, the business chooses to manage new products with the complex team structure. Each product requires a general manager and each component requires a general manager. The intention is to generate rapidly a family of new, low-cost products. The speed of the product teams is constrained by the use of common components. But the more effective the participants are at communicating, sharing databases, and resolving conflicts, the faster they can generate new and low-cost products. The ability to execute a multidimensional decision process becomes a competitive advantage in the marketplace.

Thus, the organizational design of teams can vary from simple to complex. The easiest design to manage is a series of simple teams, each with end-to-end responsibility for its task. Because each team controls its own destiny, the most freedom can be granted and the best speed in execution obtained. The teams get more complicated when the number of participants becomes too large for a single team to execute end-to-end responsibility. Teams are also more complicated when a business wants to be responsive with products but must simultaneously respond to vendors or customers. Size of group and multidimensional responsiveness both lead to the design of linkages across groups and a hierarchical conflict-resolution process. The ability to execute rapidly multidimensional team processes enhances responsiveness and achieves a competitive advantage.

In these examples, team leaders were put in place without much explanation of the integrating role. The next section discusses the design decisions involved in choosing the type of integrator and integrating roles. These roles are adopted when the teams need a full-time—and often neutral—leader. The teams will require leaders when coordination is challenging, the performance targets are difficult, and the team efforts are high priority.

Integrating Roles

The most complex aspect of the lateral process is the creation of full-time leaders. Integrating roles create the truly multidimensional organization. There is a need for these roles when a company wants to attain functional excellence, generate new products and services, and be responsive to customers. Such capacity is a requirement for some businesses in a complex, changing world.

The flexibility to deal with customers, vendors, and processes comes at a cost. First, there is the obvious investment in salaries for people who are to coordinate the work of others. The investment, however, should yield faster time to market or better customer knowledge and relationships. The second cost is the time spent resolving conflicts. Managers for customer segments, products, and functions all see the world differently. Disagreement and the inability to resolve it effectively can slow the company responses and turn the focus inward rather than on customers.

In contrast, the ability to deal with controversy and different views increases the company's ability to respond to a variety of opportunities and threats. This ability is a competitive advantage.

Design of Integrating Roles

The organizational design issues for integrating roles revolve around the power base from which the integrator will influence decisions. Managers in the hierarchical structure have authority and control of resources, but what is the power base of the integrator? How much power and influence does the integrator need? The power base of the integrator will be shaped by the following factors:

- Structure of the role
- Staffing choice
- Status of the role
- Information systems
- Planning processes
- Reward systems
- Budget authority
- Dual authority

Structure of the Role.   The ideal structure is to have the integrator report directly to the general manager. The usual practices are shown in parts A, B, and C of Figure 5.3. Because there are usually several product lines, product managers report to a product management function, as shown in version A of the figure. The product management function may have some additional people working on costs and schedules of product programs.

In a variation of this practice, the product managers report to the R&D or engineering manager. Version B shows this method in high-technology industries. Version C shows another variation, seen in consumer packaged goods industries, where products and brands have long life cycles. Both versions B and C place the product manager in a function that is dominant for the industry. The variation in version A shows a more powerful, more neutral, and more general managerlike structure, because it is not associated with any function and has direct access to the general manager. The variations are appropriate for businesses that are technology-driven (version B) or market-driven (version C). Other variations are also possible (Galbraith, 1994, chap. 5).

FIGURE 5.3. Product Manager Variations.

Version A

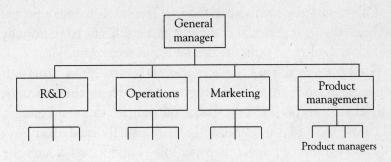

Version B

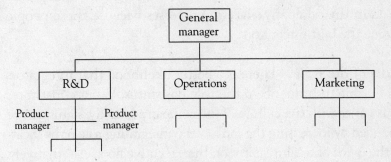

Version C

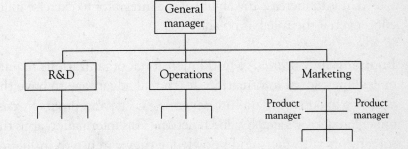

Staffing Choice. The people who play the integrator roles are the key factors in implementing the multidimensional organization. Few people who can play the general management role also have the skills to influence without authority. The key is to select people who have the interpersonal and networking skills to be personally persuasive. Technical skills are desirable but secondary.

The best way to find these individuals is to "grow" them. If people experience rotational assignments early in their careers, create their own personal networks, participate in lateral groups, and then chair a lateral group, they are usually ready to play a process integrator or project manager role. This process creates the generalist skills, builds the person's network, and teaches influence skills early on. Management's role is to select the successful participants in the company's lateral processes because these people become the best integrators.

Status of the Role. There is a better likelihood that integrators will be able to influence if the role has status. What constitutes status varies with the culture of the company. Usually, status can be enhanced by increasing the rank of the integrating role or by locating the office of the integrator on the executive floor. Alternatively, the status of the role can be enhanced by staffing it with senior people with good track records. Whatever type of status-enhancer is used, it is to increase the ability of the integrator to exercise influence, even if the role has no authority.

Information Systems. Multidimensional organizations require multidimensional information. It is a real advantage to have the capacity to convert data into revenues, costs, and profits by customer, product, geography, and function. This information arms the integrators with facts and knowledge they can use to influence others. The integrators can also contract with the line organization and then monitor the contractual agreements. Such rich data gives the integrator a cross-company visibility into a product, customer, or process that no one else has. The visibility and facts give the integrator substantial influence.

In contrast, a lack of integrated information systems presents a large impediment to companywide integration. Many reengineering projects attempt to obtain visibility across units and build databases so everyone works from the same information.

Planning Processes. The multidimensional information system can be used to support a multidimensional planning process. When based on valid data, the planning process can become the arena for focusing the natural contentions of the different perspectives for resolution. An example will illustrate this point.

A former Bell company has created market segment business units. The planning matrix for the business unit serving medium-size companies is shown in Exhibit 5.1. The functional organizations are listed across the top. The market segments managed by integrators are listed down the left side. The planning process amounts to a series of discussions between segment managers and functional managers. The managers must agree on revenues, costs, and investments in each of the rows and columns; there are always more requests for resources than resources available. The business unit general manager sets initial guidelines, facilitates crucial disputes, and manages the entire process by convening all participants. When it is completed, the planning matrix allows all managers to shoot for the same targets.

EXHIBIT 5.1. Planning Matrix.

	Sales	Marketing	Information technology	Install and repair	Network operations
Health services					
Financial services					
Governments					
Distribution					
Manufacturing					
Other					

This planning process requires information to support it. It needs participants skilled at problem solving in conflict situations. Finally, it requires a general manager skilled at managing the process and comfortable with managing conflict.

Reward Systems. The step from the planning process to the reward system is a natural one. The managers on either side of the planning matrix have agreed on their goals. It is important for each manager to make the goals in all of his or her cells in the matrix, not just in the total of all the cells (traditionally, the normal practice). Then the managers become jointly accountable and are responsible for the same goals. The information system, planning process, and reward system form an integrated package of management practices that support the multidimensional organization.

Budget Authority. Another way to enhance the integrator's role is to give it control over the budget for its product, process, or market. The organization designer specifies which budget categories and amounts are involved in order to enhance the integrator's execution of his or her coordination task.

Dual Authority. The final step in creating a power base for the integrator is to give that person authority over the people in the function. This step creates a matrix structure that contains two reporting lines. Usually one person is selected as a subproject manager, as shown in Figure 5.4.

The subproject manager alone works for two bosses. The dual authority is implemented by having both bosses participate in the joint setting of goals and joint performance assessment for the subproject manager.

Only organizations that are skilled at lateral processes should attempt the dual authority step. It creates a power balance between the dimensions of the structure. In addition, dual authority can generate its own set of conflicts. The situation can easily generate more disagreements and confusion than flexibility.

FIGURE 5.4. Matrix Structure with Dual Authority.

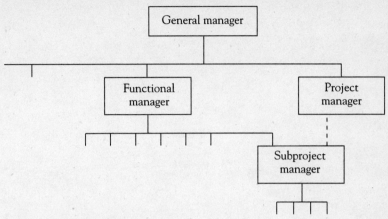

Source: Galbraith, 1994, p. 100.

The formal lateral processes of groups and integrators are powerful methods to use when management must take a strong role in the lateral organization. Through these processes a multidimensional organization is created, intended to increase the company's flexibility in responding to vendors, markets, technologies, governments, and so on. The organization is more likely to be capable of extensive communication and cooperation, and rapid escalation and resolution of conflicts. The next chapters present some additional examples of combinations of structures and lateral processes.

PART TWO:

Pathways to New Organizational Forms

6

Using Design as an Evolutionary Change Agent

In the first five chapters of this book, I presented the star model as a framework for the design process and then focused on organizational structure and lateral processes. The supporting information systems, reward systems, staff selection, and development practices were mentioned along the way. In this chapter, new organizational design structures are discussed. These designs are blends of structures and lateral processes, intended to help management face today's challenges. The chapter will focus on three design models: functional integrators, the distributed organization, and the front/back hybrid structure.

Functional Integrators

Today, companies that have achieved a reasonable size are moving toward product-based, process-based, or customer segment-based structures. Variety, change, and speed are the determinants in the choice of the new organizational structure. Lateral processes can be used to make the transition from functional structures into new structures.

For example, a company can make the transition from a functional organization to one based on market segments by using lateral processes as interim steps. Market segments may be addressed first by voluntary group processes, then by formal teams. Integrators may be a subsequent step, followed by a shift of resources to the segment managers. Through this process segment integrators become segment general managers. Along the way, the information systems, planning processes, and segment strategies develop. And at the same time managers, who may become general managers for the segments, develop. In this manner a company develops an evolutionary path from functional organization to profit-center structure. But what happens to the functions?

As the company evolves into the market segment structure, like the one shown in Figure 6.1, the functions become the lateral processes and the functional managers become integrators. (Compare this with the design shown in Exhibit 5.1 in Chapter Five.) In

FIGURE 6.1. Market Segments and Lateral Functions.

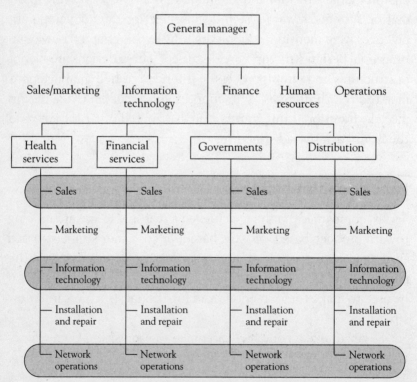

this model, decision making is moved into the profit and loss centers based on market segments, such as health care and financial services. These profit and loss centers can react much more quickly and are focused on the customers in their segment.

Each segment organization itself becomes a functional structure. Each is also a mirror image structure, having a counterpart in each of the other segments. Together, they can easily form a sales team, an information technology (IT) team, and a network team. These groups can meet and schedule educational events, share best practices, and build shared databases. The functional managers chair the teams and share those same responsibilities. The short-run operating decisions move to the market segments, while the long-run capability-building tasks move to the functional integrators. The functions focus on building the functional assets and resources for the company, which can be drawn upon by the market segments. They focus on recruiting and developing talent, creating computer-aided applications, building databases, building core competencies, developing outside suppliers for the function, and benchmarking the function against outside suppliers. They also move talent across segments to utilize fully all the company's resources.

As more and more companies face the challenges of variety, change, and speed, they are moving to segment or process structures. In doing so, they should not eliminate key functions. Instead, the functional managers should become integrators concerned with functional excellence and long-run capability building. The organization designer's task is to plan the transition and change functional managers into functional integrators, so that they have integrating and long-range planning skills.

The Distributed Organization

Another organizational type is the distributed organization. This design is increasingly being adopted in various ways by companies. Like the functional integrator model, it is a combination of structure and lateral processes. It is gaining the greatest popularity in multinationals and in companies reducing corporate staffs.

The distributed organization is created when a companywide activity is moved from the headquarters to an operating unit. The operating unit then performs that activity for the entire organization, as well as performing its own operating responsibility. The unit thus has a dual responsibility. The distributed organization is an alternative to both the centralized headquarters model and the decentralized fragmented model.

The headquarters model, illustrated in Figure 6.2, arose when some activities were essential to a business but required more scale than local or field operations could justify. Therefore, to deliver the activity efficiently, it was centralized at headquarters. In this manner, the activity was performed in one place for everyone. This model achieved scale and reduced duplication. By reporting to headquarters, the activity had a total-company view, a long-run view, and a neutral posture to serve all field units equally.

The headquarters model had some negatives, however. A centralized activity could become detached from the realities of the field and lose its sense of urgency. It usually provided a standard, undifferentiated service to different local situations. Often, the local field unit felt it could serve its own needs better, and the centralization debate began.

FIGURE 6.2. The Headquarters Model.

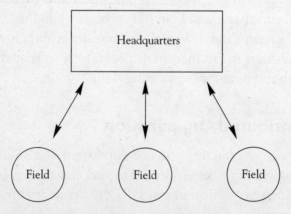

Source: Galbraith, 1994, p. 116.

Decentralization resulted when an activity was divided up and distributed to each local unit to serve its own needs. But this fragmented the activity. The distributed organization results when an entire activity is given to an operating unit, to serve its own needs and the needs of the other operating units. It represents both centralization and decentralization. But what makes this arrangement advantageous?

Often, a local field unit has the best competence in an activity. Thus, the responsibility is placed where the competence exists. If an operating unit has the best training activity in the company, why not do training for everyone in that unit? Another unit buys more semiconductors than anyone else. Why not have that unit buy semiconductors for everyone? As service businesses focus on industry segments, they move the industry segment headquarters to the office with the most expertise in that industry. For example, a consulting practice centers its automotive industry segment headquarters in Detroit, its financial services in New York, its electronics in San Francisco, its defense in Los Angeles, its government in Washington, D.C., and so on. They put the responsibility in the location where the skills and the day-to-day contacts exist. Policy and strategy are created in the most advanced markets in the industry. In each case, locating an activity at an advanced field location is superior to centralizing it at the company headquarters. Many companies follow a similar logic when placing responsibilities for core competencies. They are creating centers of excellence or responsibility for a core competency in the unit that is superior in the performance of the competency. That unit then serves the whole company.

The distributed organization can increase the motivation of the local unit. It is a compliment to be selected for an organizationwide role. It is motivating to be given an enhanced role and more responsibility. The distributed organization makes the local unit a partner in the company's performance. Indeed, the shift of headquarters activities to local units creates a peer-to-peer relationship in the company, as illustrated in Figure 6.3. The distributed organization

FIGURE 6.3. The Peer-to-Peer Model.

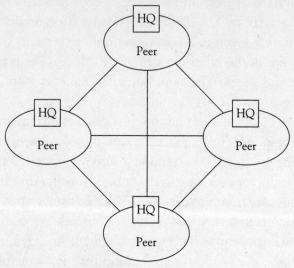

Source: Galbraith, 1994, p. 117.

is less hierarchical than the headquarters model, which is based on the parent-child relationship and concentrates all important decisions at headquarters.

The peer-to-peer aspect of the distributed organization is important in international structures. As Europe integrates economically, many companies want to shift to regional coordination and away from autonomous countries. But rather than create a regional structure in Brussels, they place regional responsibilities in each country. Therefore, each country gets important pan-European responsibility, compensating for its loss of autonomy.

A final example of the distributed organization can be drawn from manufacturing industries, where flexible manufacturing technologies permit the location of several small plants close to the customer. The customers value this, and they value the rapid response to their supply needs. But management does not want to re-create the factory overhead structure in every plant. Therefore, it distributes specific overhead tasks to each factory and each performs it for all factories. One gets electrical maintenance, another the computer systems, a third training, and so on. The overhead structure is shared, and each plant gets a companywide responsibility.

In all these cases, the distributed organization is an alternative to the headquarters model and often is superior to it. There are some costs peculiar to the distributed model. But there are also ways to manage these costs and thereby minimize them.

The main issue is the loss of neutrality in providing a key companywide service. A central unit at headquarters usually takes an unbiased total company view, and it serves local units equally or according to company priorities. But in the distributed organization, the service is provided by a local unit. What is to keep the unit from serving its own needs first and best? Or, if the local unit experiences a budget problem, what is to keep it from cutting back on companywide services to meet its budget target? The other units may get second-class service as a result. Once, the units were dependent on headquarters. Now they are dependent on fellow local units.

The best way to deal with lost neutrality is to substitute reciprocity. That is, if each of the primary local units receives a headquarters responsibility, a system of mutual dependence is created, with each local unit dependent on the others for service. If one cuts back on quality, the others can retaliate. Thus, companies stress norms of reciprocity: "I'll give you good service and I'll expect good service from you."

The distributed organization is a more interdependent and complicated model than the headquarters model. A comparison of the simple parent-child model that describes the headquarters structure with the peer-to-peer model that describes the distributed structure shows that the latter requires more communication. The distributed model probably could not be effective without modern telecommunications technology and extensive lateral processes. But the management style and communication behavior of the leader and the management team must also change. The parent-child model employs one-on-one communication with the leader. Each local unit is independent. Under the peer-to-peer model, the leader must manage the group as a team; one-on-one communication is destructive.

Below the management level, the lateral processes described earlier are appropriate. If training is the distributed activity, a training team is likely to be formed. The team may be staffed by a representative from each local unit and chaired by the manager responsible for the distributed training function. Thus there is strong communication across the local units if the activity is well coordinated.

The distributed team usually creates a companywide plan. The top management team approves the plan and uses the plan's goals to evaluate the distributed function. Often, the company uses a survey of the serviced units to test their satisfaction with the service. The company can overcome the loss of neutrality and local bias by completely designing an organization to manage distributed activities as well as by using reciprocity.

Thus, the implementation of the distributed organization is not merely placing a companywide responsibility in a local unit. It requires a complete design in the form of information and communication processes, a business plan, companywide measures and rewards, and so on. Often, the process of rotating assignments across local units is used. In short, successful implementation requires policies that align all of the elements presented in the star model.

The Front/Back Hybrid Structure

The front/back hybrid is a combination of product and market structures. It consists of a front-end structure that is focused on market segments and/or geography and a back-end structure that is focused on products and technologies. Both the front and back ends are multifunctional structures in themselves.

The front/back structure is shown in Figure 6.4, which illustrates a financial services firm that offers insurance, mutual fund, and savings certificate products. The products are organized as multifunctional businesses including every function except for sales. They

FIGURE 6.4. Front/Back Structure for Financial Services.

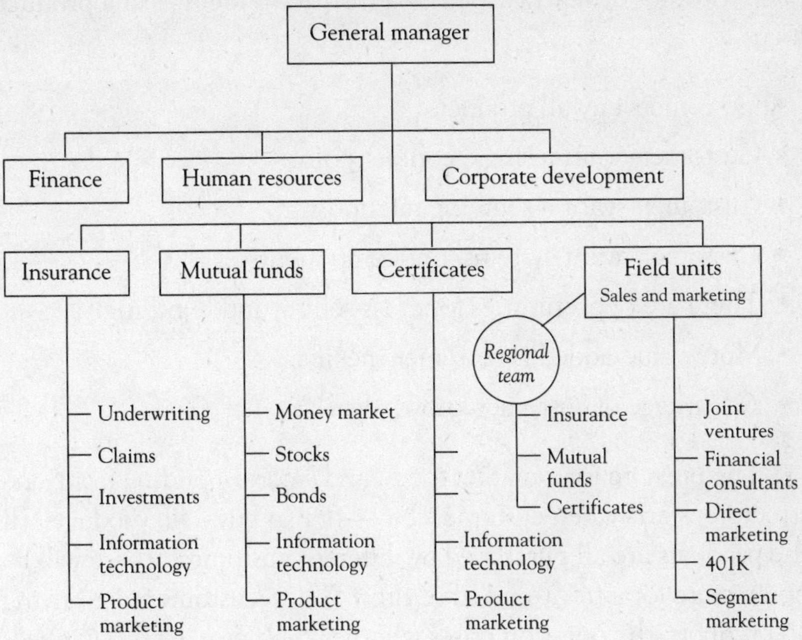

form the product-focused back-end structure. The front-end structure consists of multiple sales channels, segment marketing, and regional coordination units, which link the products and channels. Five thousand financial consultants are geographically dispersed. They provide financial advice and sell investment products. Direct mail and 800 numbers represent other distribution channels. The company recently trained financial consultants for companies offering 401K plans to their employees. All products are sold through all channels.

Successful execution of the front/back structure gives a company great flexibility. The aim is to focus the business both on markets and products; it is intended to achieve the benefits of both product and market structures. A combination of a number of forces at play in the market today is causing companies to choose this organization type. Variety, change, and speed encourage them to adopt fast-moving units based on product lines. But several other forces in addition to the standard ones can encourage the addition of a customer or market focus—a front-end focus—to a product focus:

- Customers buy all products.
- Customers want a single contact point.
- Customers want a sourcing relationship.
- Customers want systems, not components.
- There are opportunities for cross-selling and bundling.
- More value-added is customer-specific.
- Advantage of customer knowledge.

The pressure for a market focus, and a corresponding front-end structure, starts when customers buy—or can buy—all products. (If the products are all purchased by different customers, there will be no pressure for a front-end structure.) When customers are buying all products, the question arises whether each product group needs its own sales force, all of whom call on the same customer. Would it not be more economical to have one sales force sell all products to the customer? In part, the answer depends on how the customer wants to do business. Some customers have different buyers purchasing different products from the same vendor. These companies may prefer to have separate product-knowledgeable salespeople calling on separate product-knowledgeable buyers. But more customers today prefer to pool their purchases and negotiate a total single contract with multiproduct vendors. These customers want a single contact in the vendor organization with whom they can communicate and negotiate. The need for these single interfaces for customers is a force in the creation of the front-end structure.

Many customers today are adopting sourcing policies. That is, they prefer to have fewer, closer, and longer-term vendor relationships. They choose one or two vendors for a product and dedicate their entire volume to those vendors. In return, the customer may prefer—or insist—that the vendor create an organizational unit with which it can conduct its business. This unit becomes a front-end unit.

Some customers want to buy systems rather than products. Wells Fargo Bank buys products when it orders 250 personal computers from National Cash Register (NCR), AT&T's computer business unit. But Wells Fargo may want to buy a consumer banking system, which consists of many products, including desktop computers, teller terminals, automatic teller machines, high-volume transaction processors, disc drive storage, and so on. All of these products are manufactured by different units at NCR. When buying a system, Wells Fargo does not want a collection of products, it wants a banking system that works. As a result, NCR will do the systems integration for customers like Wells Fargo who do not want to do it themselves. Vendors like NCR, therefore, need a systems integration capability, which also becomes a front-end function.

On some occasions, there may be cross-selling opportunities for the vendor with customers who do not buy all the vendor's products. By packaging (or "bundling") products together for a single package price, the vendor may win a larger share of the customer's business. Cross-selling and bundling usually require a single unit in the front end to create the package for the customer.

These examples show that more value-adding activities are being done and are best located in the front-end structure. In the past, sales was the only activity organized around the customer. Today, more customer-specific software and services are being added. IBM and DEC used to have sales and after-sales equipment service in their front-end organizations. Today, they have added application software, customer education, consulting, systems integration to the front end; they will even run a customer's entire information technology function. PPG used to sell paint to the automobile manufacturers. Today, it sells paint, provides application software for choosing paints, and runs the entire painting operation for General Motors.

As the economies of developed countries become service and information oriented, companies will continue to add software and services as a source of growth. These services usually require customization for market segments and customers. As such, they should be located in the front-end structure.

Finally, many companies are recognizing that a market segment structure allows them to gain superior knowledge about customers and to form close relationships with them. If the knowledge and relationships can be converted into superior products and services, the segment focus will become a competitive advantage. The total benefits to the successfully executed front/back organization are those achieved by both market and product structures.

There are four important design issues that must be resolved in creating a front/back organization:

- Placement of marketing
- Roles and responsibilities
- Problems of contention
- Front/back linkage

The question of whether to put marketing in the front or the back end always comes up. As it turns out, marketing goes in both places. Segment or customer marketing goes in the front, focusing on segmenting the customer population. It concentrates on creating packages of products and services for segments, package pricing, channel selection, and supporting the sales force. Product marketing goes in the back, focusing on product positioning, product pricing, new product development, and product features. The two marketing activities will play key roles in linking the front and back, as we will see later in the examples.

The second design issue involves the respective roles and responsibilities of the front and the back. If these roles are not clarified, there is great potential for conflict. Just about every management decision can create contention. Who sets price? Who forecasts? Who is responsible for the inventory? The most contentious question is, Which end is the profit center? Some managements wish to emphasize one or the other. However, it is possible to design both to be profit centers, and manage them with a matrix as shown in Chapter Five. (See again Exhibit 5.1.)

The third issue is managing contention. Even if the roles and responsibilities are acceptable, there is some contention. The front end sees the world through market eyes and wants unique things for its customers. The back end sees the world through product eyes and wants scale and equal customer treatment. The discussion of the Boeing 777 in Chapter Five is typical. Management needs to create processes for using conflict to learn about customers and products, and for resolving issues in a timely fashion.

Finally, management needs to link the front with the back for key work flow processes. Orders need to enter the front and be filled at the back. Products need to be developed by the back and sold by the front. The two types of structures should not lead to two companies. A tight linkage is necessary despite the inherent conflicts. Management's time and effort in resolving conflicts and linking the front and the back are the major costs of implementing this model.

The combination of structures and lateral processes needed to execute successfully the front/back model can be illustrated with two examples, a financial services business and a consumer packaged goods manufacturer.

Financial Services Front/Back Model

The financial services company shown in Figure 6.4 appears again in Figure 6.5, but this time the key lateral processes are illustrated. This company has created the following three mechanisms for integrating the front and back and for managing inherent conflict:

- Regional teams
- A marketing council
- A career system

The first mechanism is the regional team. Regional teams are groups of people from the product and market segments who are

FIGURE 6.5. Front/Back Linkage Example: Regional Teams.

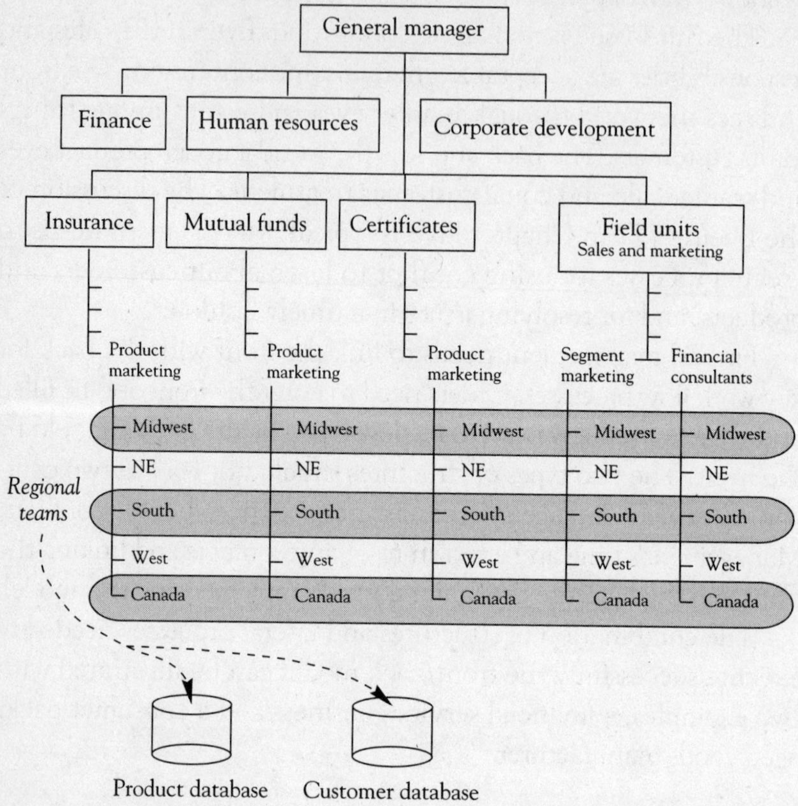

colocated. They are dedicated to groups of financial consultants in the field. The consultants get to know the teams and call them for information and transactions. One member of the team acts as a case manager in a transaction for a customer and a consultant. The case manager can complete these transactions rapidly by relying on a database with product information, on another database with customer information, and on discussions with team members. The product database also contains an expert system for issues like the insurance underwriting decision. The team member and the expert system can make underwriting commitments rapidly for about 90 percent of inquiries. Each team—armed with databases—gives the company the capability for a total-company, rapid response to consultants and to customer transactions. Each team makes the total capability of the back end accessible to geographically organized consultants on the front end. The teams are designed to support the field with information and to reduce the cycle time for inquiries and transactions. The teams can help with cross-selling the entire product line.

The second linkage mechanism is the marketing council, shown in Figure 6.6, which represents the different marketing perspectives in the company. Segment marketing from the front end uses classical analyses to distinguish different buying behaviors and the needs of different groups in the population. It requests new products and creates packages of products and pricing schemes for cross-sales. Product marketing people usually work for the mutual fund division or the insurance division. They perform the product positioning, pricing, and new product development for their product

FIGURE 6.6. Front/Back Linkage Example: Marketing Council.

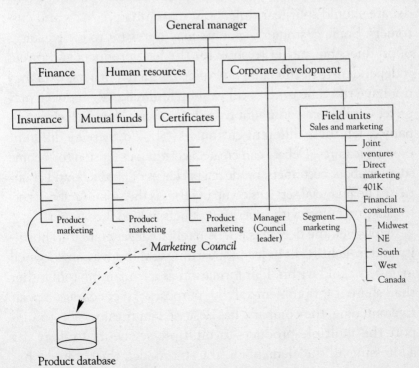

line. They keep their product line competitive with other mutual fund and insurance products. Finally, the leader of—and manager from—corporate development chairs the marketing council. The corporate development function is responsible for growth into new investment products, like foreign stocks or funds, limited partnership, and so on. It searches for new partners, acquisitions, and new channels, and it looks after the growth and development of the company. The function represents a neutral viewpoint in the front/back discussions. Corporate development searches for the best way for the company to profit from a product or channel position.

While the marketing council is the main forum for the design and discussion of the product packages, channel choices, new products, and pricing schemes, it is also the main forum for managing conflict. The segment people are enthusiastic about cross-selling and the product people are usually unenthusiastic about having their product become a loss leader. The key is to mold the debate to lead to the design and pricing of superior offerings. The debate should spur learning about matching products and customers. Some customer segments may not want to get packages of products but rather to shop for the best products and prices independently of the company offering them. Others, who may not have the time or the skill to shop for financial products, may prefer to rely on a consultant to do it for them. How does the company reach these different customers? Should there be different product features? Debate can create a continuous tension to become smarter about customers, products, packages of products, and channels. The financial services company that is the smartest about customers and fastest with superior products will be the winner.

However, the debate is just as likely to degenerate into hostility and in-fighting as to lead to learning and innovation. Council members could withhold information as a bargaining tool rather than share it for problem-solving purposes. To encourage a positive outcome, the company has designed an organization to support the multiple-products-to-multiple-segments strategy. By addressing all the elements in the star model, the company has reduced the likelihood of dysfunctional information flow. The structure and key processes appeared in Figures 6.5 and 6.6.

The third central organizational design policy is the career system, which is used to develop marketing talent. The career system starts with recruiting and selecting finance students who have marketing aptitude and are likely to be able to solve problems effectively in groups. Several schools have been developed as sources for this talent. The company provides these students with summer internships, study projects, and speakers for classes at the universities. Once hired, the new employees begin their relationship within the company on a rotation, starting with a product marketing assignment. They learn a product, then move to a regional team. On the team, they represent their products, learn other products, and get exposure to the marketplace. The system is flexible, but the preferred sequence is to move them next to segment marketing. The final assignment is corporate development. After learning products, customers, and segments, in corporate development they learn a larger perspective as well as new business development practices. From corporate development, these people can go anywhere in product marketing or segment marketing or can run a regional team. Eventually, they may find their way to running these departments—even become general managers for product lines. Thus, career systems are integrated sets of policies, from selection to promotion, that unfold over a period of years. By the time the marketing managers get to the marketing council, they have learned all the facets of the business. Training in group problem solving is part of the process, usually offered before they are sent to a regional team. The company also selects those who perform best in the group process. Thus, the people selected are likely to succeed on the marketing council. They are trained, developed, and evaluated, and selected at each stage so that they do, in fact, succeed.

The head of corporate development, who leads the marketing council, is a graduate of this career process. This person is the discussion facilitator, setting the climate for openness and problem solving. This person's knowledge and neutrality help create trust in a conflict situation.

The information system is an additional organizational design feature. It makes the same data available to everyone. The company continues to develop extensive databases and software programs that support the regional teams and the marketing council. These databases bring product, product package, customer, channel, and segment information to the problem-solving process. The visibility gives everyone the same data. The company has adopted a saying, "Everyone is entitled to their own opinion, but not to their own data."

The marketing council is linked to the management committee, as shown in Figure 6.7. The figure shows the path through which conflicts are sent up for resolution by the top management. In addition, this procedure keeps the management committee informed of the tough issues requiring top management input and policy decisions. The management committee also formulates strategy and articulates criteria that guide the marketing council's decisions.

Management has been evolving toward the creation of marketing segment profit centers. Originally, the product lines were the profit centers. They are still measured on a profit and loss basis, but

FIGURE 6.7. Linking Marketing Council to Top Management.

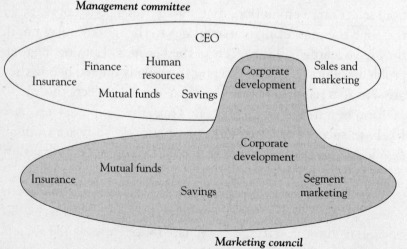

they are being joined by the segments. The segments get some package pricing freedom. The product lines get credited with a standard price, independently of what the segments do with prices. The pricing scheme eliminates some potential conflict areas. The reward system is designed to encourage a companywide rather than a parochial product view or segment view. All managers receive a bonus based on company performance rather than on product or segment performance.

Thus, this company has designed an organization with product and market focus. Through the front/back structure it coordinates the products and market segments. The career system, information system-linked committees, and the profit measure and reward system all support the management of inherent conflict. And conflict is channeled into learning about customers and new offerings for them.

Consumer Goods Manufacturing Front/Back Model

Consumer goods manufacturing companies were originally structured around product lines and brands, as shown in Figure 6.8. In the late 1980s, our example company's retail customers began to change. The volume buying and intelligence acquired through

FIGURE 6.8. Group Structure of a Consumer Products Company.

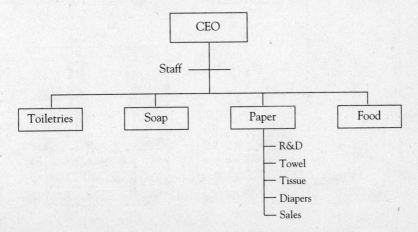

check-out counter bar code scanners at such mass merchandisers as
Wal-Mart and Kmart substantially increased their power. Some of
them demanded a single interface, along with just-in-time supply
relationships. In contrast, other retailers began to experience considerable variety in the buying habits of ethnic groups within the
regions they served. These retailers were moving in the opposite
direction from the mass merchants. They were doing less central
buying, even moving the buying decisions to the store level.

Consumer packaged goods manufacturers have responded differently to these forces. One company tried to acquire an advantage by adding a front-end structure that enables responsiveness to
all types of customers. This structure is shown in Figure 6.9, which
illustrates that both a regional structure and a customer structure
have been created as the front end of the business. The regional
and customer teams are all multifunctional and staffed by people
who come from the product groups. Customer teams are created

FIGURE 6.9. Front-End Structure.

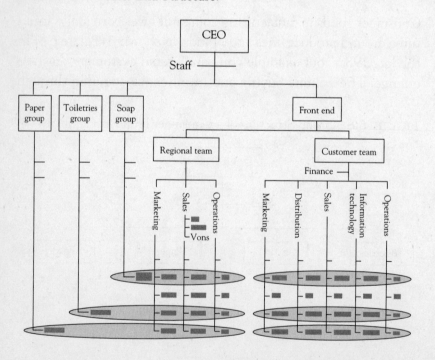

for customers large enough to justify the effort who want to coordinate operations very closely. Some customer teams are located at the customer headquarters. The teams consist of several functions. First there are the marketing people, who work with customer marketing on analyzing bar code data and using promotions to move product. Then there are the salespeople, who talk directly to the buyers at the customer's merchandising functions. Next there are distribution and information technology people, who link the logistics functions of the producer and the retailer. Sometimes factory people join the teams to discuss putting on bar codes in the factory rather than in the stores. Financial people on both sides discuss ways to speed the turnover of inventory and accounts receivables and minimize cash.

The whole cross-functional team works for a customer team leader, who is a senior manager from either sales or marketing. The leader of the entire front end is a senior manager with sales and marketing experience.

Product coordination within a customer team is accomplished by the team leader and the top functional managers, and by cross-functional teams for each product group. The product team is chaired by the marketing representative. All the product group functional representatives in the front end also communicate with their counterparts in the product groups. These representatives are on two- to three-year rotational assignment from the product groups. Their contacts within the group are kept current throughout the rotations. But in each case, there is a clearly defined interface between products and customers, using the product representatives in the front end.

The regional teams consist of three functions. The marketing function translates the product marketing message into regional versions. The sales function consists of teams that call on stores where the buying decisions are located. In Southern California, customers that are large enough to justify a team are such retailers as Boys Market and Vons. One store in Monterey Park serves a largely Taiwanese population. Products must appeal to ethnic Chinese and be in Chinese packaging. The same retailer in Malibu serves the specialized beach community with health foods. The local variety of customers requires responsiveness on a local level. The operations function works with the stores' operations people to set up displays and stock shelves. The functional people on regional teams also can form product teams and communicate with their counterparts in the product groups.

Some customers prefer to do business as they have in the past. For these customers, the company sends salespeople from the group sales forces. The soap salesperson talks to the soap buyer; salespeople from the paper group talk to the paper buyer. So salespeople can be organized by group (as they have been traditionally), by region, or by customer. The company has maintained product specialization at the salesperson level, but it has organized them simultaneously by product group, region, and customer. A rotational assignment process develops them to see all three sides of the issue and maintain personal networks.

One strength of this front/back design is that it allows the company to do business *the way the customer wants to do business*. Different customers prefer different relationships. Another strength of the design is the clear identification of product people and product teams in the front end. These groups can communicate and coordinate within the front end and between the front end and the back end. The structure makes it easy for the customer, but it can be complex for the producer. The same conflicts as described before exist between customer teams and product lines. In addition, the different interfaces with different customers makes things difficult to coordinate. But if the company can manage the conflict and the complexity, it will have achieved a competitive advantage. Competitors cannot easily copy and execute the entire front/back organization.

These two examples of the front/back model give some idea of the richness of this design option. The first illustrates the total design approach by using a package of all of the policies illustrated in the star model. The latter example is a good illustration of a front/back organization that is structured to generate products and manage the complexity of doing business the way different customers want to do business.

In addition to representing current trends in organizational design, the functional integrator model, the distributed organization, and the front/back model illustrate combinations of structure and lateral processes. Another organizational design currently in use is called the virtual corporation. It is described in the next chapter.

7

Creating a
Virtual
Corporation

The virtual corporation, sometimes called the networked organization, is another form of organization that is becoming popular. It is created by extensive contracting out of activities once performed in-house. The new information technology facilitates the virtual corporation by allowing independent firms to join together in networks, which then act as if they are single corporations. There are some compelling reasons to choose the virtual corporation design, but there are also some negatives.

What Is a Virtual Corporation?

Virtual corporation is another fashionable term in the business press. The virtual corporation is sometimes defined by what it is not. It is the exact opposite of the vertically integrated corporation. Instead of covering all the activities a business comprises— from raw material to the ultimate consumer—the virtual corporation contracts out for all activities except those in which it is superior. As a result, a network of independent companies— each doing what it does best—acts together as if it were virtually a single corporation. Hence the name. But why is the virtual corporation popular?

When duly qualified, it is an option with considerable merit. The virtual corporation is a reflection of the trend to contract out. The traditional corporate model was for a company to own and control all activities that created value for its customers. But today, companies recognize that they are not—and cannot—be best at everything. Yet, in today's competitive market, a company must be best at everything. The virtual corporation can provide the answer, as companies perform what they do best and seek to acquire or become partners with other companies that do what they do best in order to get superior total offering for the customer.

Also favoring the virtual corporation is the issue of size. Some suggest that in today's economy—characterized by variety, change, and speed, as discussed in the other chapters of this book—size is no longer an advantage, and may even be a disadvantage. Some would say that the future belongs to the small entrepreneurial niche firm. And, indeed, in an increasing number of situations small is beautiful. However, in some industries small niche firms are being taken over by larger firms with more scale and deeper pockets; in the automobile industry, Jaguar, Saab, and Mazda are examples. Peter Drucker has proposed a compromise by suggesting that medium is the best size. The medium-size firm is not too large to move quickly and not too small to get scale. He suggests that this medium-size firm is the real strength of German industry.

In this book, our position is that the virtual corporation provides the ultimate answer. It can be large when it is an advantage to be large and it can be small when it is an advantage to be small. For example, it is an advantage to be large when buying; volume discounts and better terms can be secured. Thus, the independent companies within the virtual corporation can pool their purchases, and one company—usually the lead company—can buy for all companies. Benetton, the Italian fashion house, takes this approach. It contracts out most manufacturing to about 350 small firms and buys the materials for all of them. Benetton has become the world's largest purchaser of wool thread and exercises considerable leverage in that market. However, it is good to be small and independent when fast, flexible responses are called for. The labor-intensive fashion sewing and packing operations are performed for Benetton by twenty- to twenty-five–person firms. Collectively, these small companies can handle the variety and flexibility needed to supply rapidly changing fashion merchandise to a fickle market.

Thus, the virtual corporation is able to gain scale without mass. Yet Benetton and other virtual corporations can be both large and small, depending on which is advantageous at the time.

Flexible sourcing is another advantage to using networks of independent firms. For example, in the past decade five different printing and four different storage technologies have been used for personal computers. By contracting out for components, Apple has avoided building a dot-matrix printing factory and a floppy disc drive factory. If flash memories replace hard disc drives, Apple can quickly shift to the new storage devices by establishing a new source. The virtual corporation is thus an advantage in fast-moving, changing industries.

The virtual corporation is made possible largely by the new information technology. Benetton has designed an international telecom network that ties together all of its franchise stores and all of its subcontracted factories. These 6,000 franchises and 350 factories interact via an extensive, worldwide telecommunications network that a Fortune 500 company would be proud to own. But instead of owning it, Benneton holds together the network through telecommunications and intelligence.

But the virtual corporation, like any organizational form, has its disadvantages. The greatest disadvantage is the possible loss of proprietary knowledge. In order to work with other companies, information has to be exchanged. But when important information is given to others, potential competitors are created. For example, Apple taught independent software vendors about the Macintosh's operating system so that they could write application programs that would run on the Mac. One of those vendors was Microsoft. Microsoft did, indeed, write programs for the Mac, but it also incorporated what it learned into its own operating system, Windows.

Once Windows 3.0 appeared, Apple had lost its competitive advantage. Similarly, Schwinn contracted out its bicycle manufacturing to a Taiwanese firm. After learning the U.S. bicycle business, the Taiwanese firm sidestepped Schwinn and went directly into distribution through mass merchandisers like Wal-Mart. Schwinn is just now emerging from Chapter 11.

Another disadvantage is that the more activities are contracted out, the more profit and value-added given to others. Conversely, the more things a firm is good at doing the more value and profit it can keep to itself.

A third possible negative is loss of control over parts of the business. If a disagreement arises with another firm in the network, the manager cannot fire the firm; one firm cannot force another to do something. Issues must be negotiated. Disagreements can lead to endless discussions. There is no tiebreaker to stop the discussions and initiate action. But, as we will see, a company can minimize these negatives by getting skillful at the partnering process, which will be described later in the chapter.

Designing the Virtual Corporation

The design of the organization, as usual, follows from the business strategy, but in this case the business strategy is the partnering strategy. What is unusual is that the partnering strategy is established independently of the organizational structure. Partnering is equally likely for functional, product, process, or market structures. The key organizational design issues that need to be addressed are the following:

- Partnering strategy
- External relationships
- Partner selection
- Partnership structure
- Supporting policies

Strategy is, of course, a crucial element—as it is in any organizational design. In the following discussion, though, the element that will need the most consideration is external relationships; this is the make-or-break issue in the virtual corporation's design.

Partnering Strategy

The business strategy of interest is the partnering strategy. Although the company's product/market strategy influences structure and internal lateral processes, as described in earlier chapters, the partnering strategy affects the lateral relationships between companies in the network. This strategy delineates the company's role in the network and determines the activities to own and perform and those to contract out. The organizational design will coordinate and influence the contracted-out activities.

Company Role. A company can play different roles in a network, from specialist to network integrator for the entire business. A specialist performs one or a few activities and provides the service to everyone. A network integrator attempts to coordinate the activities performed by many firms, including itself, in order to create value for the ultimate customer.

Specialists attempt to become best in the world at the few activities they perform. SCI manufactures printed circuit boards, for example. It manufactures more boards and invests more in process R&D than anyone else. Then it sells its services to network integrators in all industries in all countries. Why would any company want to manufacture printed circuit boards when it can buy them from SCI? Federal Express does the same for distribution; Automatic Data Processing (ADP) performs all payroll processing. Each is an expert and usually the lowest-cost provider in the specialty.

The network integrator is a firm that coordinates the decisions and actions of the companies making up the network. This firm takes the lead and manages the network as if it were a vertically integrated company. It formulates the strategy for the overall network, chooses member firms, and links them together with a telecom system. Nike, like Benetton, mentioned earlier, coordinates the work of independent factories in Asia and of retailers in all the markets that it serves. It coordinates all the work, from raw material to the customer, even though the work is performed by others.

A firm may choose to perform the entire integrating task, as Nike, Benetton, and Apple do, or it may integrate portions of the activities. If it integrates a portion of the total business, it may choose to link with peer firms integrating complementary portions.

Thus, the company's partnering strategy starts with the choice of role that it will play in the virtual corporation.

Activities of the Integrating Role. For companies taking on an integrating role, there is a choice among the activities it performs, owns, and controls and those it contracts out. Usually, a company performs those activities that the customer finds important, those for which there are few outside suppliers, those that involve scale, those that integrate the members of the network, those that influence the brand, and those that give the firm an opportunity for competitive advantage. Commodities and input from plentiful or superior suppliers are contracted out.

A difficult choice must be made when an activity is important in the eyes of the customer, but outside suppliers are superior. The company can then invest to improve its own capability or form a close relationship with an outside supplier, hoping to manage its dependency and perhaps learn some of the needed skills.

Boeing is an example of a network integrator. Over the years it has managed the systems integration function and the difficult customer relationship, and, in terms of product, the cockpit—where all systems converge—and as much of the wings as it can retain. The rest is subcontracted to specialists around the world (which helps sell airplanes to airlines owned by governments). Boeing has thus strategically positioned itself to integrate the business, from raw material to the customer, while performing about 20 percent of the actual work.

External Relationships

Once a company has chosen its role in the network and decided which activities to perform and which to contract out, it needs to design processes to coordinate the activities performed by others. Communication and joint decision processes are needed to manage the interdependence between the companies in the network. These external relationships are similar in many ways to the internal lateral processes of a firm and the types and amounts of coordination among them similarly vary. Thus the task of the organizational designer is once again to match the types and amounts of coordination with the appropriate types and amounts of external lateral relationships.

The design choice is again governed by the type of external relationships. These vary from a market relationship between buyer and seller, to contracting between parties, to sourcing and alliance arrangements, to equity relationships, to outright ownership. The continuum is shown in Figure 7.1, where the relationships are linked with the amount of coordination required and the amount of dependence on the outside firm. The relationships at the top are the cheapest and easiest to use. As the designer proceeds down the list, the relationships become more complex and require more management time and effort. The designer should proceed only until the point of coordination required by the partnering strategy is reached.

FIGURE 7.1. Types of External Relationships and Coordination Requirements.

Relationships	Relative strength	Coordination	Dependence
	Weak		
Market		None	Zero
Contract		Occasional/some	Minimum
Sourcing/alliance		Substantial	Moderate
Equity		Great deal	High
Ownership		Great deal	Very high
	Strong		

Markets and Contracts. Markets and contracts are standard mechanisms for mediating economic transactions. The figure shows that relationships mediated by markets require little coordination and communication between the parties. Indeed, the purchase of commodities from spot markets takes place between buyers and sellers who remain unknown to each other. Markets are used to secure products and services that are standard and freely available.

The contract relationship is somewhat more involved. The buyer and seller communicate and negotiate terms periodically, but there is little subsequent contact unless exceptions arise. Contracts come to pass when the items being acquired are not standard and are not always available. Some items may need to be customized, others may be standard—like dynamic random access memories (DRAMs) for personal computers—but are subject to shortages. A contract guarantees the source of supply for the length of the contract, and specifies the customization.

Sourcing and Alliances. Sourcing and alliance relationships require more coordination. Sourcing involves a contract, but it involves a closer and longer-term relationship. Usually the parties reveal their long-term plans to one another and participate in jointly developing products and services. For example, automobile companies are becoming more like network integrators and forming sourcing relationships with suppliers. Ford may choose TRW to supply all passenger safety equipment, like seat belts, air bags, and so on. TRW then has to share its technology and development plans in order to be chosen. Ford shares its car development plans with TRW, which may design safety equipment unique to Ford. TRW may have to invest in special equipment in order to make the unique products. Ford may then make TRW the sole supplier of the total volume to justify TRW's investment.

This kind of sourcing relationship has several characteristics. One is the substantial customizing by the supplier for the unique advantage of the customer. In return, the customer makes the customizer the sole or preferred supplier, as in the Ford/TRW example, which reduces the risk for the supplier and grants the volume to pay for the effort. Sourcing relationships also involve a great deal of communication about future plans and coordination of product and service development. The parties become partners, jointly developing the unique product. There is usually a formal product development team with representatives from both parties. As with internal lateral processes, there will be an integrator (a product manager from the vendor), so that the product development team can span both companies. The partners will share the same computer-aided design system and design information. After the product is designed, the ordering and supplying will be done electronically as well. Thus, sourcing relationships are fewer, closer, longer-term relationships.

Although the terminology is not standard, similar relationships between competitors (as opposed to between suppliers and customers) are usually referred to as alliances (or "teaming," in aerospace). The parties in an alliance also exchange information and commitments and jointly perform an activity and share the outcome. For example, IBM and Siemens formed an alliance to develop jointly the process technology for manufacturing sixteen megabit DRAMs. Each subsequently produced and marketed the product independently. Motorola and Toshiba formed an alliance to exchange technologies. Toshiba provided manufacturing process technology for DRAMs; Motorola provided microprocessor technology. The technologies were transferred during joint development of products using the technologies.

In each case, a development team or teams are staffed by both partners. There is an integrator role to coordinate the joint effort and manage the relationship. A great deal of coordination and communication between the partners is essential to perform the joint activity.

Equity Relationships. The equity relationship is so named because it involves the transfer of equity. There are three main types of arrangements for the transfer of equity. In some cases it is the network integrator taking a minority shareholding in a supplier. Ford, for example, invested in Cummins Engine for a 20 percent stake and in Mazda for a 25 percent stake. The amounts vary, but the network integrator takes a substantial—although a minority— position. In other types of equity relationships, each member takes a small stake in the others. For example, Swiss Air, Delta, and Singapore Airlines each bought 5 percent of the other in order to seal their alliance and coordinate schedules. These cross-share holdings are used in alliances among equals. The most involved equity relationship is the joint venture. Here, a separate company is created with its own equity, which is usually split more or less equally between the parties.

Thus, the equity relationships can be joint ventures, cross-share holdings, or minority stakes, each with varying amounts of equity involved. They are alliances with a lot of control and a significant investment. There may be as much need for coordination and communication as in an alliance, but one or both partners may be more dependent and vulnerable. The exchange of equity symbolizes greater commitment and a long-term commitment. The equity relationship is usually more difficult to unwind than an alliance, which may even have a termination date.

Equity relationships are used when the dependency cannot be covered by normal contractual terms and conditions. In the example of Ford and TRW, an equity relationship may not be necessary. TRW is vulnerable in this relationship because Ford may reveal TRW's technology to another supplier and demand a lower-cost proposal from that supplier. Ford is vulnerable because TRW could slightly modify the Ford product and sell it to General Motors or Honda. The parties could, however, agree to nondisclosure clauses and noncompetitive products for a two-year period. At the end of two years, all competitors will have reverse-engineered the product and discovered the technology, anyway. So if each partner adheres to the contractual agreement, the vulnerabilities of all are protected.

Enduring advantages, those that are critical or cannot easily be copied, usually need more protection. In certain cases, one partner may have an enormous incentive to use the proprietary information. In circumstances such as these, an equity exchange aligns the partners' interests and gives them more control over the relationship. The equity is intended to be a long-term bond of trust.

Ownership. Equity is not a guarantee that the partnership will not fall apart. It increases the probability of success at a cost. The ultimate control is 100 percent ownership of an activity. If the vulnerability is too great for one partner, or the opportunity for profit too large to share, one of the partners will purchase the other.

The application software unit of Apple is a good example. When the Mac first appeared, little application software was available for it. So Apple started its own software unit, which created MacPaint and MacDraw. Outside software houses became interested in creating software for the Mac, but they were reluctant to share information because Apple's in-house unit was a competitor. Apple decided to make the unit, called Claris, a separate company but maintained a minority interest. But just before Apple's public stock offering, it pulled Claris back into the company. The reason? Microsoft had introduced Windows, and Claris was the software company with the most experience writing programs for Windows-type operating systems. With ten times as many computers capable of running Windows as Macs, Claris's incentive was to write primarily for Windows and secondarily for the Mac. But as a wholly owned unit of Apple, Claris would support the Mac first. Apple needed full control of Claris to align its interests with those of Claris.

So two factors, coordination and vulnerability, drive companies to choose more complex forms of relationships. Alliances and sourcing relationships are adopted to achieve the coordination needed to execute customization and joint development; markets and simple contracts are insufficient by themselves. But working jointly with other companies increases the vulnerability of the firm. Equity exchanges reduce the vulnerability and increase the firm's commitment and control. The combination of increased coordination and reduced vulnerability drive organization designers to choose the more complex relationships.

Partner Selection

The choice of partner is crucial in alliances and equity relationships. (There is less dependence and vulnerability with market and contract relationships.) Firms that are skilled at alliances and equity ventures continuously and thoroughly evaluate potential partners.

The first priority when selecting a partner is to understand the potential partner's strategic intentions. Ford's intention may be to develop TRW as its safety equipment partner. Another auto manufacturer may use a partnership to learn TRW's technology and create its own internal capability. It may then use its internal capability to supply its own needs or to negotiate lower prices from TRW, having stripped it of its technical edge. Knowing these intentions in advance is the key to partner selection. Other factors include compatibility of goals, values, styles, time horizons, and so on.

Corning, a skilled partner, continuously locates partner candidates and assigns them to the company's officers. The top manager then investigates the candidate; a consulting firm analyzes the company and its history. Corning has found that it can learn more about a company's values during adversity. It investigates the company's behavior during an event such as a plant closure, a hazardous waste spill, and so on. Corning then gets to know the candidate's management, inviting them to speak at meetings or attend the annual officers meeting; it has them bring their spouses and gets to know them informally. A small joint project may be next. In this way, people at various working levels get to know one another. Each contact is a test. If a candidate passes all of them, Corning may try an alliance. If successful, it may try a larger alliance, evolve toward an equity relationship and, eventually, a joint venture. The selection process is continuous and thorough.

The selection process requires a lot of time and effort from management. However, this degree of up-front effort is characteristic of successful partnering. As the old saying goes, "You pay me now or you pay me later." Issues not discovered in the courtship will arise later in the partnership. They are more difficult to solve then, and the relationship more difficult to dissolve.

Today, the evaluation of partner candidates is getting easier. More companies now have a partnering history that can be examined. Indeed, in the future, being seen as an attractive partner will be a requirement for competitiveness. Thus, gaining a good reputation as a partner actually controls certain temptations to behave opportunistically in alliances. More and more companies are investing in the up-front courtship process to find appropriate partners for longer-term relationships.

Partnership Structure

Alliances and joint ventures are joint activities that need to be structured. There are three types of structures for joint activities. In the *operator model* one partner takes the management responsibility for the joint activity. In the *shared model* responsibility is divided between the two partners. And finally, and primarily, in *joint ventures*, the joint activity can be autonomous.

The basic model for the partnership structure is shown in Figure 7.2. The two-partner structures shown in the figure may be any of those already discussed in Chapter Three. The alliance (or venture) itself is probably a functional structure focused on developing

FIGURE 7.2. Partnership Structure for Sourcing, Alliances, or Joint Ventures.

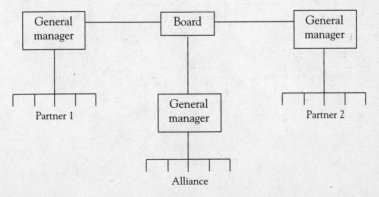

and supplying a product, service, or technology. Members from both partners form a board to supervise the activity.

The operator model is used in sourcing arrangements and sometimes in alliances and joint ventures. In the Ford/TRW example, TRW probably serves as the operator and manages the product development effort. Ford contributes some people to work on the product and several managers to serve on the board. But the alliance manager and key functional managers are from TRW. The decision-making orientation is illustrated by the shading in Figure 7.3. The board acts much like a normal board of directors, reviewing work, approving investments, and agreeing on the selection of key people.

In the General Motors/Toyota (NUMMI) joint venture, Toyota was the operator. Toyota wanted to learn how to manage in the United States and how to partner with United Auto Workers (UAW). General Motors wanted to learn Toyota's production system. Both objectives were served by having Toyota manage the joint venture even though ownership was 50/50.

The Motorola/Toshiba relationship involves an exchange of operator roles. Toshiba was the operator on the DRAM alliance, where it was the expert. Motorola was the operator on the microprocessor alliance, where it was the expert.

FIGURE 7.3. The Operator Alliance Model.

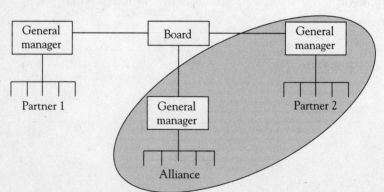

The operator model has been more successful than the shared model. It makes one company responsible. It minimizes conflicts. It leads to faster decisions. This model is preferred when one partner has the capabilities to manage the efforts and also works best when the role can be rotated between partners, as in the Motorola/ Toshiba example.

The shared model, used in many alliances and joint ventures, is preferred when each partner brings a complementary skill. When Ford and Mazda form an alliance to create a new car, they share the responsibility. For small cars, Mazda has the product development engineering design, and manufacturing skills, while Ford has the styling, finance, and marketing competencies. They divide the work based on skills and share overall management responsibility. The focal point of decision-making shifts, as illustrated in Figure 7.4.

The shared model is characterized by a small and active board. Usually, the board consists of four or five—but no more than seven—people. It is staffed with two managers from each partner and the alliance general manager. This general manager comes from one partner and one of the managers from the other partner chairs the board.

FIGURE 7.4. The Shared Alliance Model.

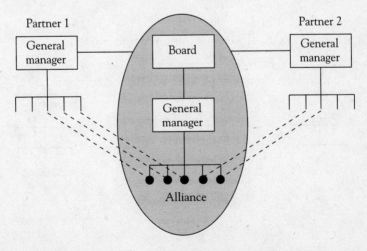

A difficulty of the shared model is the potential for conflict among the partners or indecision. Indecision is likely if managers in the partner organizations interfere instead of using the board as the decision-making focal point. But if the partners are skilled at alliances and joint ventures and if the board is active, the partnership can capitalize on the combination of the complementary skills.

The third type of structure is the autonomous model, shown in Figure 7.5. In this model, the decisions are made by the venture itself, which becomes more independent of its parents. Usually the autonomous model is adopted by joint ventures. A venture usually begins by using the operator or shared model and evolves into the autonomous model. As the venture becomes successful and grows its own talent, it becomes less dependent on its parents. The board becomes an ordinary board; the major decisions are made within the venture. The benefit is that the venture can then act more quickly to changing business situations.

Supporting Policies

The design of the virtual corporation is completed with the creation of supporting policies corresponding to the two remaining elements of the star model: the selection and development of people

FIGURE 7.5. The Autonomous Joint Venture Model.

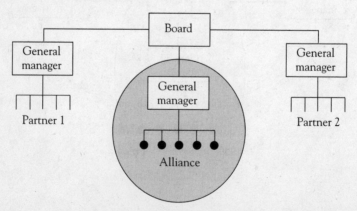

and the reward system. Both are enlisted to create behaviors, values, and norms that support the partnering process.

Many of the same skills that facilitate lateral internal processes facilitate processes between companies. Particularly key are an ability to influence without authority and a facility for working with people from different cultures. Often, people can graduate from participation in internal processes to external ones.

The other "people issue" is the selection and development of people who can deal with the dilemma of partnering. That is, they must reveal information and cooperate with partners but must not reveal certain critical pieces of information. Part of this people issue is choosing individuals who can walk this fine line and be comfortable. The other part is training them to understand the aspects of the company's strategy and core competencies that should not be revealed. As more and more people work in direct contact with people from other companies, this training will become crucial.

The reward system needs to be augmented in order to encourage employees to look for the win/win outcome. Managers at Corning all tell stories of bosses who have reprimanded them for not looking for a benefit for the other partner. Partnering has to be good for both parties. Effective companies promote the "seeing of the situation" through the partners' eyes.

For example, one company is reevaluating its partnering approach. It has always tried to win in negotiations. And last year it won a very nice royalty agreement from its Japanese partner. But this year, it is not celebrating: the royalty is so favorable that the partner has no incentive to fulfill the partnership. The company is currently renegotiating so that both partners can profit from the relationship. Thus the reward system needs to make a constant search for the win/win outcome.

The virtual corporation is a new name for groups of companies that contract out to one another. The network of companies that is formed acts collectively as if it were an integrated company.

In a virtual corporation, the key choices for the individual firm are its role in the network and the specific activities it will perform, own, and control. The organizational design choices are the type of relationships among firms, the firms to work with, the structure of the joint efforts, and the development of employees to participate in partnerships.

8

Leading and Integrating a Networked Organization

Chapter Seven described the virtual corporation as a network of independent companies that acts as if it is a single corporation. In order for independent companies to act in this way, their activities have to be coordinated. This coordination is provided by the firms that choose to perform the role of the network integrator. A firm can choose to integrate a subset of firms or the entire set of firms comprising the network to perform the role of the network integrator.

This chapter describes how firms can qualify for and execute the integrating role. To set the framework for the integrator role, the concept of an industry value-added chain is also described. The network integrator coordinates the activities across the value chain for a particular industry.

The Industry Value Chain

Every industry has a value chain, a sequence of activities that transforms raw materials into the end product or service. Figure 8.1 shows the value chain for the automobile industry. The sequence of activities begins with the conversion of raw material (such as steel) into parts (brake drums), the conversion of parts into

FIGURE 8.1. The Value Chain for the Auto Industry.

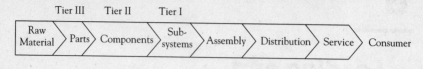

components (front wheel brakes), and the conversion of components into subsystems (antilock braking systems). The assembly process creates the automobile, which is distributed to dealers. Finally, after-sales service completes the product and services that are purchased by the final consumer.

The virtual corporation consists of independent companies that perform activities along an industry's value chain. The integrator coordinates the flow of work. The integrator usually chooses the firms that constitute the virtual corporation and assumes responsibility for the corporation's maintenance.

Historically, the original equipment manufacturers (OEMs), like Ford and General Motors, vertically integrated and owned all of the activities along the chain except for the dealers who distributed and serviced the final products. Henry Ford even integrated backward to the point of running his own steel mills at the River Rouge complex. Today, OEMs are "vertically disintegrating" for the reasons described in Chapter Seven. For example, Chrysler adds only about 30 percent of the total value to the cars it makes and subcontracts out the remaining 70 percent.

However, Chrysler would still like to take on the task of integrating its supply network from raw material to the final consumer. It contracts out whole subsystems when it can. Tier-one suppliers integrate the value chain from raw material to the OEM. For example, Chrysler would like to have tier-one suppliers handle the entire braking subsystem (including front-wheel, rear-wheel, power hydraulics, and antilock braking systems). These tier-one suppliers would be network integrators for their portion of the value chain from raw material to delivery to the OEM. They might even jointly share in the warranty system for the brakes and participate in supplying after-sales service. In this way, Chrysler assumes the responsibility for integrating the entire value chain so as to service the ultimate consumer. The tier-one supplier takes responsibility for integrating a portion of the value chain, or subchain, in order to service the OEM. Both play the role of network integrator for their portion of the value chain. There are also tier-two and tier-three suppliers who could integrate from raw material to the tier-one supplier.

Companies choose to play the integrator role because there are still benefits to integrating vertically. When work flows are coordinated, all firms along the chain can minimize inventories and speed product flow. When information and forecasts are shared, suppliers can plan and coordinate capacity investments. With joint product and service development, the firms can speed new products and services to market. By working together, they can reduce duplication and total network costs. These are the benefits of vertical integration. However, many firms have discovered that common ownership is not necessary for all to work toward common goals. They can get around this by acting as if they are vertically integrated, with some firms taking the leadership, or integrating, roles.

Performing the Integrating Role

A leadership role usually allows a firm to earn superior returns. But the leadership role must be earned. The integrator must have the skills and abilities to lead the other firms. The integrator's leadership must result in better performance for all firms along the chain in order for them to accept the integrator's leadership. Often the position of the leader changes along with changes in the industry structure. The next sections explore the conditions that permit some firms to take leadership and play the integrating role.

Negotiating Leverage

The virtual corporation is held together by constant negotiation. At Boeing every new airplane represents an opportunity to renegotiate the relationships in the network. At Chrysler every new car platform, at Nike every new shoe style represents opportunities to renegotiate. In addition to being a good negotiator and knowing how to do deals, the firm that plays the integrator role must have a power base from which to negotiate.

Very often the integrator uses its size for leverage in buying and selling with other members of the network. Chrysler is the largest entity in its network. It uses its buying power to its own and the network's advantage. For example, Chrysler will influence one supplier to specialize in front wheel brakes, another to specialize in rear wheel brakes, and both to reduce redundant research and development (R&D) and other expenses. The network thereby lowers its total costs and duplication and Chrysler awards its volume to those who comply with its suggestions.

The integrator may also create a power base by maintaining options when dealing with many suppliers and customers. Nike spreads its manufacturing among fifty factories in Korea, Taiwan, China, and Indonesia. Benetton uses 350 small manufacturers and sells through 100 agents and 6,000 stores. Whether they use the leverage or not, the suppliers need Nike and Benetton more than the integrators need the suppliers. But as we shall see shortly, the integrator also needs trust and credibility. The integrator is better off not having to use its leverage. The benefit of leverage, like veto power, lies in its threat and not in its use.

Leverage can also be gained through proprietary technology. Apple acts as a network integrator and uses its size and its proprietary technology to gain leverage. It integrates the work of twelve thousand small software publishers who write software that runs on the Macintosh. These software developers depend on Apple to use its size to get shelf space for them in retail outlets and to make joint sales calls on large users. But Microsoft also writes software for Apple. Apple also uses Sony and Canon as suppliers. In each case, Apple uses its superior design technology to maintain dependence and get negotiating leverage. Apple designs its own disks and printers, and leads Sony and Canon, who are willing to learn from

Apple. Apple protects itself with nondisclosure agreements, non-compete clauses, and rapid movement to new technologies when the agreements expire.

Knowledge and Information

In order to integrate all activities in the network, the integrator must have knowledge of and information about all activities in the value chain. It must have the capability to use this information to integrate the network activities to achieve superior collective performance when compared with other networks, collections of independents, or vertically integrated companies. The integrator uses its knowledge and information to formulate strategies for the virtual corporation, to conceive of winning products and services, and to coordinate work flows, costs, and prices within the network.

The new information technology offers many opportunities for creating information to integrate the value chain. The integrator needs to know where to find opportunities for cost reduction and value creation anywhere along the chain. As mentioned earlier Benetton sells through 6,000 independent stores and manufactures through 350 independent small factories. But it has created an information system that records bar code data from sales in stores and coordinates the work flows to keep all stores supplied. Each factory has a personal computer that is wired into the system and gets work flow information from all the stores for all of its products. With this information system, Benetton has total visibility into the work flow from raw material to consumer.

Benetton also has ten stores and two factories of its own. Through these facilities it can understand the cost structures and margins of each stage of the value chain. The ten stores are located in key trend-setting markets. Thus Benetton stays informed to negotiate with members of the network, to coordinate work flows to benefit the customer, and to see fashion trends for new products. Benetton also manages the working capital for its network; thus the network's costs are lower and its cash flow faster than that of The Gap's network or of other competitors.

Another way to capture information and profit from that information is to embed intelligence in the products offered. By placing microprocessors and value-added software in products, for example, the product manufacturer can profit in several ways. For example, elevator manufacturers can sell service contracts and the product can be monitored continuously from remote sites. Repairs can be made to the software without on-site personnel to monitor it. When sensors detect a breakdown, repair crews can be dispatched. In this way the manufacturer can control the service and reliability of the product and coordinate a network of repair businesses. This kind of service may be provided for any piece of capital equipment or durable good that requires after-sales service.

The information can also result in improved product designs. With access to product performance data, better products, better software, and self-correcting features for frequently failing components can be designed. The information allows the manufacturer to integrate into the network data directly from the customer. Similarly, 800 numbers bringing customer inquiries and customer information give manufacturers data usually reserved for the service and repair stages in the value chain.

Thus, the integrator of a value chain is located along the value chain where scale is highest and access to information most easily obtained. This location varies with the industry and can change over time within an industry. As an example, the book publishing industry's value chain is shown in Figure 8.2. The raw material for the publishing industry is authors. Authors may be represented by agents, who contract with publishers, who edit and produce the authors' books. Printers create the books themselves, which are distributed and sold through bookstores. In the past, the chain was integrated by the book publishers. They searched for authors and ideas that they believed there was a market for. They knew how to match potential authors and the interests of the marketplace. They took the risks. They managed the promotion. They were usually

FIGURE 8.2. The Value Chain for the Publishing Industry.

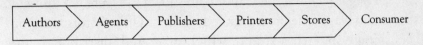

the largest entity in the chain, with the possible exception of the printers.

But today the small bookstore is being replaced by superstores. The leverage has shifted to these large stores, without whom publishers cannot have a best-seller. Waldenbooks, for example, has been trying to integrate the chain. With its presence in many markets, bar code data, and direct customer access, Waldenbooks thinks it is better positioned to match a market and an author than most book publishers are. It can go directly to best-selling authors like Danielle Steele, Sidney Sheldon, and James Michener and strike deals that give Waldenbooks a three-month exclusive and bypass the publishers altogether. Waldenbooks also thinks it can promote books better, design jackets better, and suggest better titles and prices. In short, it is contesting the integrating role of the book publisher in the publishing industry's virtual corporation, using its buying leverage and knowledge of the market to integrate the chain for books in a manner that could be more effective.

Financial Capability

Very often the integrator brings its financial capability to finance projects or deals for other members of the network. At first Benetton had difficulty getting Italian banks to finance its small store and factory owners. So it established a factoring subsidiary to finance the accounts receivables of its stores. It established finance and leasing subsidiaries to finance the inventories and equipment purchases of its suppliers. Thus instead of being an owner of all activities along the value chain, Benetton is the banker to independent companies.

The example of the movie business further illustrates how the integrator role can shift to different points along the value chain.

The movie business in Hollywood was always dominated by the studios. They integrated the value chain shown in Figure 8.3. Initially the chain was vertically integrated by the studios. Actors and writers signed on with a studio, which marketed, distributed, and financed movies that were shown in the studio's own theaters. A combination of the antitrust laws and the phenomenon of the independent producer broke up the studios. Yet the studios still integrated the chain by controlling distribution, knowing what would sell, and financing expensive film projects. They became skilled at creating limited partnerships and ownership structures for individual films and packages of films.

FIGURE 8.3. The Value Chain for the Movie Industry.

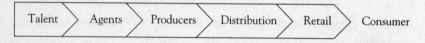

Today this integrating role too is being contested. Superagents, like Creative Artists Agency (CAA) run by Michael Ovitz, can put together a film package on their own. Using talent that it represents, CAA can sign writers, composers, directors, producers, and actors and create its own film. It can hold the rights to the work and then hire the studios to distribute it. If the superagent is big enough to create a whole package and is positioned to know which actors and scripts will match the public's taste, it is able to integrate the value chain.

The next step, which is being taken by CAA and the William Morris Agency, is to create an investment banking capability for financing and risk taking. Studios will have to compete with superagents even at the earliest stages of film development.

Credibility

In addition to all of the preceding assets, it is advantageous for the integrator to have the trust of the other network participants. These participants are independent companies; they choose to follow the leadership of the integrator. The integrator must use its superior size, information, and capital to benefit the network rather than to exploit it. Therefore, the integrator looks for network opportunities, sees the mutual fate of all the network's members, and searches for win-win situations.

Among the Big Three carmakers, Chrysler is the most skilled at playing the role of integrator. It has an expression, "My enemy is my supplier's costs, not my supplier's margins. Therefore, what can I do to help my suppliers reduce their (and ultimately my) costs?" Chrysler wants its suppliers to be financially healthy and to expand when Chrysler expands. Chrysler will include its suppliers on its steel contract. For an amount equal to the supplier's volume to Chrysler, the supplier will pay the same price as Chrysler does for such commodities. Chrysler will then negotiate with the supplier about how to allocate the savings due to the discount. As a result, Chrysler profits from the success of its tier one suppliers.

The integrator that has the trust and confidence of its network members greatly reduces its negotiating costs measured in the time and efforts of its managers. The credible integrator is more likely to get better information from its partners and better, more flexible terms and conditions on its contracts. It can avoid constraining conditions and covenants. Thus, once again, being seen as a good partner is a competitive advantage.

Responsibility for the Network

The integrator needs an awareness of and a willingness to fix or perform all activities in the network. Delivering value to the customer depends on all the network participants along the value chain performing well. The integrator (usually the owner of the brand) assumes responsibility for all activities, whether it performs them or doesn't perform them. If some activities are not performed well, the integrator takes corrective action. These actions begin with assistance to the weak member but may end up with its expulsion from the network. The integrator may send help in the form of people from its own organization to provide consulting and training. The integrator may arrange visits to superior performers in the network. Ultimately, the integrator replaces the poor performer or performs the activity itself.

Once again, Apple provides a good example. In Europe, Apple distributes through franchises called Apple Centres. These Centres experienced difficulty finding computer-literate salespeople. So Apple undertook the responsibility to do the university recruiting for them. Further, Apple created Apple University, which does the training that each franchisee could not do on its own.

In another example, Coca-Cola distributes its product through independently owned bottlers. Often a third or fourth generation owner will not be competent or will take out cash rather than grow market share. Ultimately Coke buys out the poor performer, fixes the franchise, brings in new leadership, and resells the equity. Thus, although integrators do not perform all activities along the value chain, they assume responsibility to see that all activities are performed well.

Brand Management

The integrator usually assumes the responsibility for managing the brand of the product or service. There is often intellectual property or a design feature that distinguishes the product or service and a brand franchise is necessary to capture higher margins. Consumer goods companies, like Nike, Benetton, Apple, and Nintendo, all manage the brand and the advertising for their products. They also manage all activities along the value chain to ensure the value of their brand franchises.

The virtual corporation requires some management of the independent members. The firms that play the role of network integrator for all or portions of the value chain provide that management and provide leadership. Management achieves efficiencies along the value chain that neither vertically integrated companies nor uncoordinated independents can achieve. Although these efficiencies are shared along the value chain, the lion's share goes to the integrator. Thus, there is some competition to play the role. Firms most likely to execute the leadership are those with leverage, knowledge, and information of the entire chain; access to capital; credibility among the members; a willingness and ability to be responsible for the chain; and brand management capabilities. The competition is continuous and characterized by shifts along the chain as industry structures change.

This chapter completes the description of the organizational designs that are emerging in response to today's management challenges. Chapter Nine discusses how to go about conducting an organizational design effort and introduces a useful tool for defining authority and responsibility.

9

Organizing the Continuous Design Process

The organizational design tools described in these chapters can make a substantive difference in the efficient operation of a company. But taking information from page to boardroom can be an arduous journey. This chapter describes issues to be on the lookout for and methods to help manage some of the stresses that always seem to accompany change.

The Organizational Design Process

Organizational design is a process; it is a continuous process, not a single event. To keep the process continuous and current, a sequence for changing design policies is required. But the right mind-set in managers is also required.

Leaders must learn to think of *organizing* as a verb, an active verb. Organizing is a continuous management task, like budgeting, scheduling, or communicating. Too often, organization is seen to be synonymous with structure, which changes infrequently. In today's world, a good organization is one that lasts long enough to get you to the next one. A continuously changing business environment requires a continuously changeable organization to keep pace.

We begin our discussion with the time line shown in Figure 9.1, which illustrates how today's company evolves toward the future organization. Not surprisingly, the future organization is guided by the future strategy, with the addition of desirable values and attributes along the way. The future strategy applies to the company two, three, or five years down the road, depending on the predictability of the business environment. This long-range strategy provides the criteria for choosing the future organizational type, along with the values that the company believes to be desirable. For example, some companies want to become the "employer of choice" for certain segments of the population. These values also become criteria for evaluating alternative design choices. The different priorities assigned to the various criteria also help determine the design choice.

At the other end of the time line is today's organization. It should be assessed or diagnosed by how well it fits its current

FIGURE 9.1. Continuous Organizational Design.

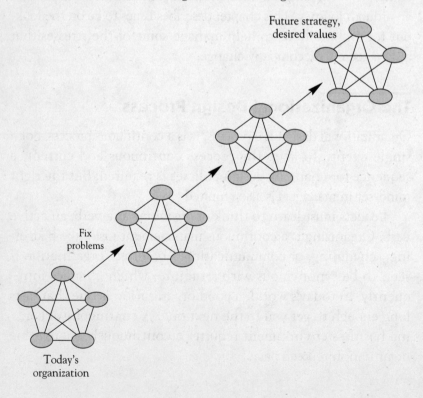

Future strategy, desired values

Fix problems

Today's organization

business environment. Management needs to make design changes to fix what is not working today, but in a manner consistent with the organization of the future.

Other intervening design steps can also be placed on the time line. Information systems always seem to set the pace of change and they take long development times. With this exception, the trend today is toward accelerated change, "high velocity" change. Still, developing new systems and training people can take longer than anticipated.

Design Sequence

As managers look at the star model they often ask, "Where do I start?" My preference is indicated by the layout of the star's components: begin with strategy and move clockwise, returning to some policies as you get smarter about the desired behavior needed to implement the strategy. The preferred sequence of design steps is shown in a more detailed manner in Figure 9.2.

As noted, strategy is the place to begin. The strategy sets the basic direction and generates the criteria for choosing the other policies. Next, the departmental structure that best executes the strategy should be designed. The department type (based on geography, functions, products) communicates priority in addressing the strategy. It forms the vertical structure across which the key processes will take place. If the structure is functional, the processes may be designed to be cross-functional new product teams or cross-functional work flow process teams.

In order for vertical structures and lateral processes to mesh effectively, the roles and responsibilities of functional managers and process teams need to be defined and clarified. Who is responsible for pricing, forecasting, or personnel assignments? Key people can then be selected for the various roles. Mismatches can lead to a redefinition of the roles and responsibilities.

Once chosen, these people will need the relevant information. Information systems design follows. The appropriate performance measures can now be deduced and rewards designed to motivate

FIGURE 9.2. The Preferred Design Process.

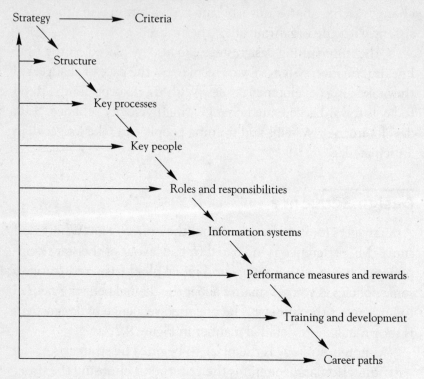

appropriate behavior. Then the people can be trained and developed for their new roles in the organization. Finally, the designers can think their way through the career paths, in order to grow the talent needed for the various roles in the structure.

Although this process has a logical flow, it can encounter practical problems. What if the strategy is not clear? If it is not clear, the structure should not be changed. In turbulent industries, such as the multimedia industry today, the future is unknowable. Under such circumstances the designer should use the current structure or adopt a generic functional one and focus on processes. Processes are like organizational software; they are flexible and easily changed. So the designer should create some processes (teams, task forces) that (1) manage the current business, (2) lead to learning about the evolving new business, and (3) allow the formulation of strategy as learning proceeds. Once the strategy crystallizes, a change to the appropriate structure is in order.

What if strategy always changes and never crystallizes? In this case, the designer continuously uses processes. The structure serves as "the homeroom" as people move from team to team. Reconfigurable project teams are the essence of the flexible organization.

Under some circumstances, different areas of the star model may seem to provide better starting points than strategy does. For example, people in the company may be complaining about compensation. In this case, the design process should begin with rewards because they will provide momentum and energy for change. However, to design a new reward system, one must determine what kind of behavior is needed—and this question invariably leads back to strategy. Thus, the strategy provides the focus no matter where the starting point is. Actually where one starts is arbitrary; it is more important to touch all policy areas on the star than to start at the "right" place. The star model and strategy eventually provide the guidance.

How Do I Choose the Right Structure?

The plan for changing the organization emerges by plotting the sequence of changes on a time line. As noted, the first changes should work to fix current problems and, through a sequence of steps, evolve in a continuous fashion to the future organization. The choice of structures and processes is made essentially by assigning a priority to the possible dimensions of the organization—functions, geography, products, markets, and processes. The priority comes from the strategy and, particularly, from the diversity of the business.

The decision process, therefore, begins with an analysis of the diversity of the business, as illustrated in Figure 9.3. The first cut at structure is determined by whether the business is service- or product-based, and whether it produces a single line of products and services or multiple lines. This framework contains four possible basic starting points, because a business may consist of a

FIGURE 9.3. The First Step in Choosing a Structure.

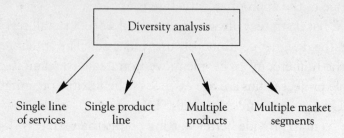

single line of services, a single line of products, multiple product lines, or multiple market segments.

Let us start with examples of service businesses that offer a single line of services—an advertising agency and a group of pizza restaurants. The decision process for such companies is shown schematically in Figure 9.4. Following the diversity analysis model, the next question for a service business is whether it serves multiple and distinct geographical areas. If the advertising agency serves a single region, it will probably adopt a functional structure, the typical structure for a single-line business. For the ad agency, the functional structure would be one in which specialists like writers, artists, TV programmers, and so on, would form departments. Account executives in another department would manage the customer relationship. The remaining functions would be administrative departments, like human resources and finance.

The organization designer then moves to the next priority in the decision process. For the ad agency, the customers would come next. An agency's work is to put together advertising programs for existing customers or to propose campaigns for new ones. These programs would be developed by formal cross-specialty teams. Because the requirements of a customer program are constantly changing, the agency would not want to "hardwire" the cross-specialty or customer teams into the organization. The account executive would coordinate the team and provide the link to the customer. Thus, the organization for an agency would consist of specialist groups (functions) that serve as homerooms for the

FIGURE 9.4. The Decision Process for Single Line of Service Businesses.

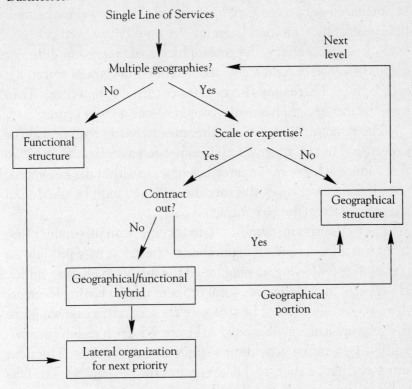

development of specialists, functional experts, and specialty tools. However, the actual work of developing a customer program or targeting an advertising campaign would be performed by cross-specialty teams.

The third priority would be processes for managing money and people. The finance and human resources departments act as integrators and design the processes for managing these phenomena. They work informally with key people in each department and with formal, cross-departmental teams when changing the design of budgeting or recruiting processes.

In this manner, the designer moves through the decision process by considering all the different organizational dimensions and assigning priorities to them based on the strategy. In the case of a business providing a single service in a single geography, the structure is functional, with customer programs and administration processes the key management processes to be designed. The answer to the multiple geographies question in Figure 9.4 would have been yes.

For the pizza chain, the geographies could represent different markets—urban or rural areas, or different ethnic groups within the geographies. There may also be different local competitors. Thus each distinct geographical area could become a profit center.

The remaining issue is whether any activities require scale or expertise. That is, are any activities needed to deliver the service that cannot achieve minimum efficient scale within the geographic area? If the answer is yes, then another question must be asked. Can the scale or expertise be contracted out?

Let us use the restaurant chain serving a single product line (pizza) as an example. The purchasing function may provide an opportunity for buying supplies for all restaurants in all geographies. However, if all suppliers are local or there is little buying leverage, there is no scale effect. The structure chosen in this case would be the geographical one illustrated in Figure 9.5. Each region becomes a single geography providing a single line of services. The next structure decision shifts to the level below the geographies. The flow chart in Figure 9.4 shows that the decision process returns to the functional organization below each geography and the previous analysis is repeated.

FIGURE 9.5. Geographical Structure.

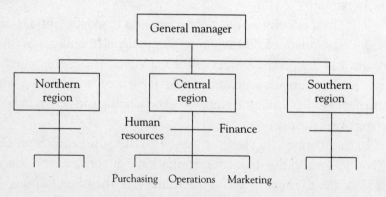

However, there may be some vendors who can supply all regions. By concentrating purchases with these vendors, significant savings in food costs may be achieved. If buying is a key skill not to be contracted out, the purchasing function probably will be centralized. The resulting structure would be a functional/geographical hybrid, like the one shown in Figure 9.6. As with all hybrids, linkage between the two dimensions is critical. In this example, cheese and flour are purchased centrally and other ingredients are purchased locally. Cross-geography linkage is provided by the central purchasing function, which chairs a team of local purchasing people from each region.

After the purchasing, or scale function, is broken out and organized centrally, the remaining activities—operations, marketing, and so on—are organized into three regions as before. Also as before, each region is organized functionally.

Another possibility illustrated by Figure 9.4 is that of the need for expertise, such as real estate expertise. The choice and purchase of sites for new stores, as well as the sale of redundant sites, requires specific real estate knowledge. Rather than have each regional manager, who is not an expert in real estate, choose and buy or lease sites, a central activity like purchasing could be created. Or the activity could be contracted out to local professionals. When contracting out for scale or expertise, the decision process returns to a regional structure, as shown in Figure 9.5.

FIGURE 9.6. Hybrid Functional/Geographical Structure.

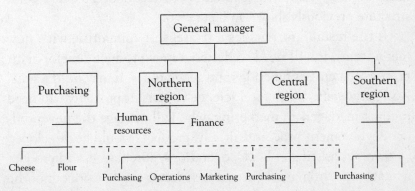

Thus, a business offering a single line of services could result in a functional structure, a geographical structure, or a functional/geographical hybrid. The key strategic issues are whether the service is delivered across multiple, distinct geographies and whether any of the activities require scale or expertise that is greater than can be provided in a single geography. The functional structure is complemented by a lateral organization focused on customer programs and projects. The geographical structures are usually complemented by lateral coordination processes for functions and products or services. The type and amount of lateral processes vary with the function and amount of new product or service development.

The example of the purchasing function was noted previously. In one case it yielded buying leverage and was centralized (Figure 9.6). The central function then played the integrator role and chaired the cross-geographical purchasing team for coordinating other policies and practices. An operations integrator can be used to chair an operations team when there are frequent changes in operating technologies and practices. A team can share best practices without an integrator if operation technologies are not very dynamic. There may also be a marketing integrator if there is a common brand shared across the geographies. The central marketing group will manage the brand along with cross-geographical advertising and promotion. A cross-geographical marketing team would coordinate best practices and manage promotions that cross several regions. Human resources and finance would be treated similarly. Figure 9.7 shows the lateral processes added to the hybrid structure previously shown in Figure 9.6.

If the restaurant pursues a strategy of competing with new menu items, it will need to design a new product development process that crosses functions and geographies. It may need a small R&D unit staffed with food science experts. It probably will need product managers in marketing, who will manage the new product development process. Initially, products would be developed by teams consisting of R&D, operations, purchasing, and product management from marketing. These teams would work out of the

FIGURE 9.7. Hybrid Functional/Geographical Structure with Functional Integrators and Teams.

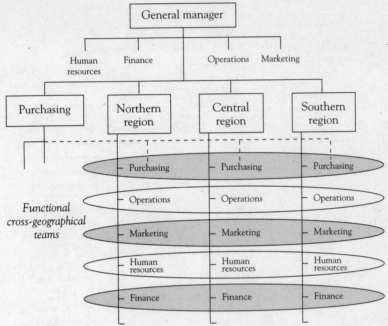

corporate headquarters, as shown in Figure 9.8. The products would be rolled out to the regions and the responsibility transferred to cross-functional teams within each region. When a product is launched and becomes a standard menu item, the teams would disband or prepare for the next new item. In this manner, the single line of service business develops capabilities for executing strategies requiring a geographical, functional, and new product or service focus.

The possible structures for single product line businesses are shown in Figure 9.9. Single product line businesses have traditionally been functionally structured. Today, the key questions are whether the business competes on speed and requires fast cycles. If speed is required, the structure is based on work flow processes, such as order fulfillment, new product development, and so on. Here functions would get second priority but would be coordinated with

FIGURE 9.8. Hybrid Structure Plus Product Teams.

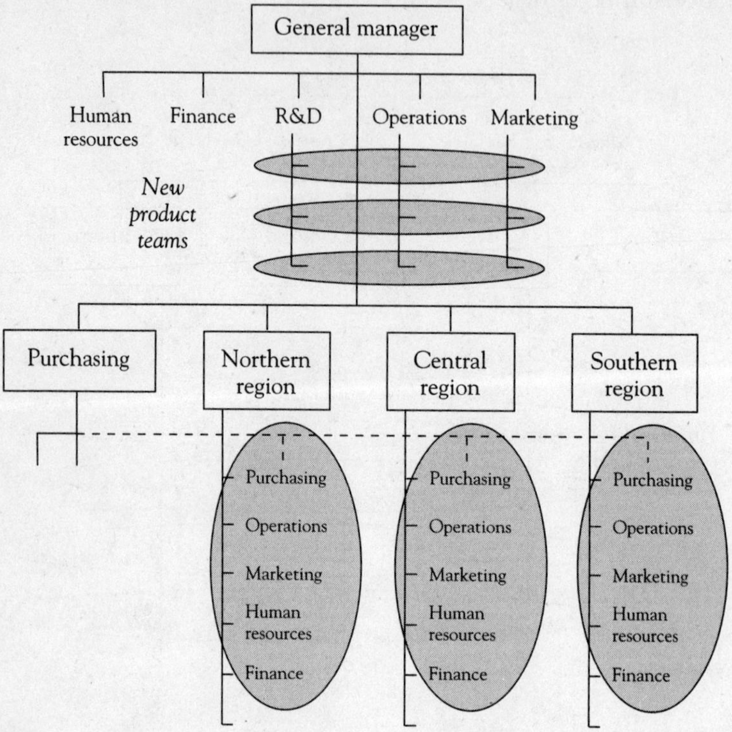

lateral management processes. If long cycles are acceptable, the structure would be primarily functional with lateral work flow process coordination.

It is also possible for a service business to require a geographical structure. If the product has a low value-to-transport cost ratio and low minimum efficient scale levels, it is possible to create geographical profit centers, as shown in Figure 9.5. Cement and cardboard packaging businesses are examples of such service businesses. The analysis for the service business can also apply to the single-product business and will not be repeated here.

The diversity analysis might conclude that the business is a multiproduct one, like Gillette, which makes razors and blades, personal care products, pens, and small electric products such as Braun razors. Similarly it could conclude that the business is a multiservice one,

FIGURE 9.9. Possible Single-Product Business Structures.

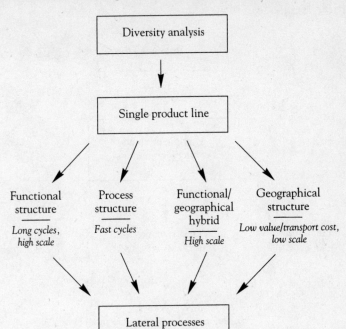

like Merrill-Lynch, which provides investment banking, brokerage, and trading services. Or it may indicate a multimarket business like Citibank, which engages in consumer banking, commercial banking, and other services for high individuals with a high net worth. The decision process for these types of organizations is shown in Figure 9.10. The typical outcome is a multibusiness, multiprofit-center structure based on different things: product lines for Gillette, markets for Citibank, and service lines for Merrill-Lynch. Each profit center is itself a single line of business.

At this point, the analysis for single-line businesses can be applied to each profit center. They may be organized by function, process, or geography and the other dimensions will be prioritized and organized laterally.

The other possibilities are the hybrids, either functional or front/back. The functional product hybrid was shown and discussed in Chapter Three. The functional geographical hybrid was discussed

FIGURE 9.10. Decision Process for Structure and Processes of Multiple Businesses.

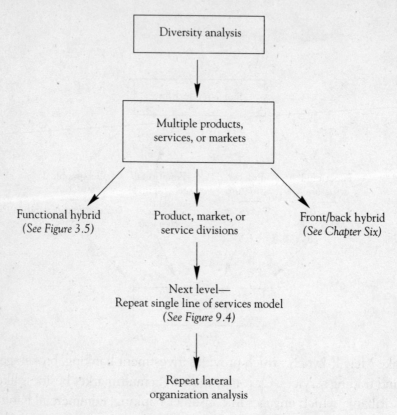

earlier in this chapter and is shown in Figure 9.6. The front/back model for products, markets, and geographies was discussed in Chapter Six. After the basic structure is chosen, the front and back portions are analyzed to determine if they should be functional, process, or geographic. The lower-priority dimensions become the basis for the lateral organization.

Thus, the process begins with a diversity analysis, which helps the decision maker choose the basic type of structure. Once the multiple profit center model has been defined, whether it is products or services, markets or geographies, or hybrids, a second analysis determines the structure within each division. For example, a multiproduct business may be organized at the top level by product units, but each product unit may be organized functionally, geo-graphically, or by process, depending on the analysis derived within each product division. The analysis continues to examine all dimensions and to specify types and amounts of lateral coordina-tion. For example, for the single-line business restaurant that oper-ated in different, distinct geographies, the structure was regional divisions. Each region was further structured into functions. Lateral coordination across regions for each function took place through teams and integrators. New product development teams were the third dimension of the pizza restaurant business structure when it decided to compete with new menu items.

The completion of the design process should lead to a choice of structure and of lateral processes. The next step is to define more clearly the roles of the managers in the new organization. The responsibility chart described in the next section is a key tool in this next step.

Roles and Responsibilities

The process of defining roles and responsibilities begins after the structure and lateral processes have been designed. After making any change to the organization, each employee will want to know "What is my role?" Whether working with lateral processes inside the company or executing alliances across partner companies, the question always is "Who is responsible for what?" One of the most useful tools in implementing any organizational design is the responsibility chart, shown in Exhibit 9.1.

The structure defines which roles need definition. It is best to stick to only two levels of structure for this exercise. As shown in the chart, the roles form the (vertical) columns. The key decisions that these roles will execute form the (horizontal) rows. These deci-sions are likely to be contentious. They are the ones around which the turf and territory issues are likely to surface.

To create the chart, the people who play the roles listed in the columns are interviewed. They suggest which decisions should be

EXHIBIT 9.1. Responsibility Chart for a Financial Services Organization.

Roles \ Decisions	Sales	Segment marketing	Insurance	Mutrual funds	Marketing council	CEO	Finance	Human resources	Regional team
Product price									
Package design									
Package price									
Forecast	A	R	C	C	C	I	I	X	X
Product design									

listed. It is best to list about thirty-five decisions. Too few decisions will not provide the clarity needed to know who is responsible for what. Too many will require a laborious effort to define the roles; it will seem too bureaucratic.

After the matrix is completed, the people playing the roles fill out the matrix individually. They answer the question, "How should we make decisions in the new organization?" In order to complete the matrix, they need a language to describe the different ways that a role can affect a decision. Four is the usual number, with no formal role a fifth option:

R = Responsible

A = Approve

C = Consult

I = Inform

X = No Formal Role

The person who is responsible for making a decision is given an R in the appropriate box. The segment marketing group, for example, is responsible for the forecast. That is, the segment marketing people initiate the process, collect the information, maintain the database for it, and arrive at a forecast.

Ideally, there would be one R for each row and no entries of any other kind. However, in multidimensional organizations, other types of roles are at play in joint decisions. For example, the sales function does not do the forecast but it must approve it. That is, sales must concur with the forecast before segment marketing can implement it. Therefore, sales's box gets an A. If there is no agreement, segment marketing and sales must negotiate. Sales cannot overturn the forecast, but it must agree with it. If there is still no agreement, the issue is raised to the CEO for resolution. Others may not be required to approve a decision, but they must be consulted by the responsible party. The C placed in the box for the general managers and the marketing council signifies that segment marketing must get input from them before making a commitment. However, once having gotten their input, segment marketing can decide what to do; it does not need their agreement. It only needs to consult with the parties who have been given Cs.

Finally, some roles do not need to be involved in a decision before it is made but do need to know the outcome afterward. For example, the finance function needs to know the forecast so that it can make cash forecasts and so on. But finance does not need to participate in the forecast itself. Finance needs to be informed, so it is given an I in the appropriate box. Others have no formal role in this decision. If those given an R want to involve them, that is fine. These people receive an X.

After each role occupant has completed the chart, everyone meets, usually off-site, for a half day or a full day to discuss and reach agreement on the role assignments. Usually, the results of the individual matrix assessment are displayed. There is almost always complete disagreement. The disparity motivates a lively discussion. A facilitator then proceeds, decision by decision. For each decision, the discussion revolves around why a person should participate. What value does that person provide? Is it worth the complexity and possible time delay to have him or her participate? This discussion is the real value of the exercise. People begin to talk about how they will work together. They teach one another about their roles. In the end, there is usually consensus and a completed matrix. If there is no consensus, then the CEO must say, "Okay, I have heard the arguments. Most people prefer this way. Let's try it and see if it works. We'll review the outcomes in three months. Next decision."

In either case, in the end the matrix is completed. To define a role, one simply proceeds down the column under the role title. The entries become the assignments. The process educates the participants and creates consensus about roles and responsibilities. The matrix provides the clarity needed in the flexible, ever-changing organizations of today. If another change is made to the organization, the chart is simply redrawn. It is a tool that can be frequently used and disseminated throughout the organization.

Design Effectiveness and Implementation

How can the effectiveness of an organizational design be gauged? There are two aspects to effectiveness (Figure 9.11).

Organizational designs are effective when they achieve a strategic fit. A strategic fit occurs when all of the policies in the star model are aligned with the strategy and reinforce one another. A strategic fit means effectiveness because congruence among the policies sends a clear and consistent signal to organization members and guides their behavior.

Also contributing to effectiveness is the amount of commitment among organization members to implement the design. Management needs to follow a design process that builds this

FIGURE 9.11. Design Effectiveness.

| Strategic fit | X | Commitment to implement | = | Effectiveness |

commitment. Neither fit nor commitment is sufficient by itself; both are needed.

Most of this book has been devoted to the process of achieving a strategic fit. In this last section, I will briefly describe a process for building commitment to implement the design. This is a process that I have developed and used over the years. (For a more complete presentation of these implementation processes see Mohrman and Cummings, 1989.)

The Organizational Design Process

The process discussed in this section is one of teaching people how to design their own organization. The organizational design process, shown in Figure 9.12, begins with the general manager working with his or her direct reports, hereafter called the executive team. These are the people whose organization is to be designed. The process is presented to them and shaped by them to fit their circumstances. The purpose of the discussion is to get the executive team comfortable with an open design process.

Development of Criteria and Alternative Structures

The first step is a kickoff workshop, which lasts about three days. The first half day includes an educational presentation, during which the ideas in this book are presented and discussed. The purpose of the presentation is to give everyone a shared framework and language, as well as some ideas about current best practices. There is no limit to the size of the group that attends this first session. Usually everyone who will participate in the design effort is either present or connected by video conference. Often the session is videotaped for viewing by those who are absent or any others who wish to see the presentation and discuss it with their work group. Books are provided when they are pertinent.

The remaining two or two and a half days are devoted to the executive team or a subgroup of it, which becomes the design team.

FIGURE 9.12. The Organizational Design Process.

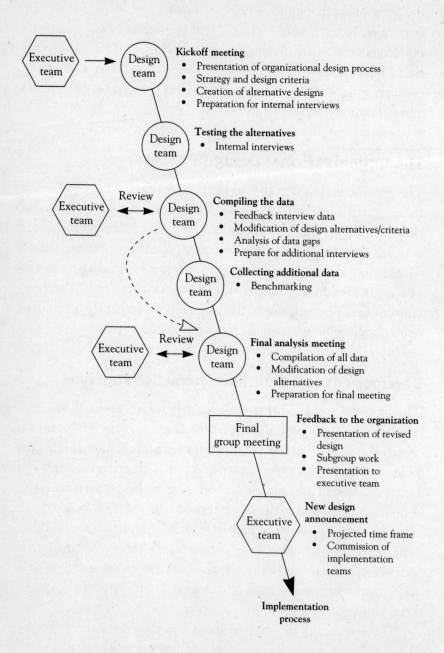

After a question-and-answer period covering the issues of the morning presentation, the design team reviews the business strategy. From the strategy, team members derive the design criteria that the new organization is to satisfy. The criteria should be concrete statements about how the organization will behave. Examples are, "We will deliver Product X no later than twenty-four hours after the customer has ordered it," or "We will generate a minimum of five viable new product ideas each month," or "We will improve quality by a factor of ten times each year." After coming up with about twenty-five criteria, the design team discusses them. It uses some procedure with which team members are familiar to choose and rank the criteria. The result should be about five key criteria, which will guide the design.

The strategy is then used to frame a future organization toward which the company will evolve. The alternatives to be designed are those that fix today's organizational problems and move the company toward tomorrow's desired organization.

The design team's next task is to create alternative designs using the process described earlier in this chapter. The alternative designs include structure and key lateral processes. Each alternative is discussed; the positives and negatives of each are listed. Depending on the size of the team and the number of alternatives, the design team can form subgroups or remain together to carry out this procedure. The design team then arrives at from one to three alternatives with which they are comfortable. These alternatives must then be tested on the rest of the organization. The purpose of the test will be both to inform the organization of what the design team is considering and to solicit input.

The remainder of the workshop is taken up with planning and scheduling the interview process (for the test) among organization members. Part of this process is developing a standard interview format to define the presentation and questions to be asked. In some cases, when an organization is under cost-reduction pressure, for example, the organizational design process is perceived as a head-count reduction exercise. If this is the case, the design team members must be prepared to address those concerns during the interview process.

Testing the Alternatives

The design team members, either singly or in pairs, interview the sixty to seventy people who will be affected by any organizational change. Team members interview people in a part of the company for which they are not responsible. There are two reasons for this. First, team members learn about a new part of the company and, second, they tend to get more open responses to their questions. During the interview, the team member presents the design team's current thinking about the strategy, the criteria they derived from the strategy, and the alternative organizational structures (including any lateral processes) that they are proposing. The interviewees ask questions and critique the alternatives from their own vantage points. If they are not pleased with a particular alternative, they are asked to propose a countersolution. This is the interviewee's first opportunity to respond to the criteria or the alternative structures.

The interviews can take place in many ways. Ideally every organization member is interviewed individually, face-to-face. However, this is not always possible or practical. Key individuals should always receive individual attention, but others may be interviewed in groups or through video conference. The design team makes the trade-offs between time, resources, and the people to include. Often outside consultants can provide help and additional resources for interviews.

Compiling the Data and Modifying the Design

After completing the interviews, the design team must consolidate and analyze the responses. The team should gain a good idea of where the organization stands at this point. Is there an emerging consensus for all or parts of the alternatives? The design team then makes modifications to the criteria and the structure alternatives or to the emerging, preferred alternative, based on the organization's input. At this point, the design team can review progress with the executive team, or other higher authorities, as necessary.

A decision is usually made at this point to go directly to the final meeting, or to conduct another round of data collection and analysis. If there is an emerging consensus and time is critical, a company is likely to go directly to a final meeting. However, there may be several "sticking points" that require further work. These issues become the agenda for the next phase of design.

Benchmarking and Collecting Additional Data

One effective tool is the benchmarking visit. Other companies that have wrestled with the controversial issues or have solved them can be visited. These visits are best conducted at the stage when the design team knows what it needs to know more about. The groups visiting other companies can include design team members and others who may benefit from the experience.

Other workshops may be used to address specific topics. Experts from inside and outside the company may be convened to solve problems around an issue. The design team itself may probe more deeply into the issues.

Compiling Data and Preparing for the Final Meeting

The design team convenes to review the results of the second-phase analysis and to revisit the criteria and design alternatives. Modifications are made based on what the team has learned. At this point, the team tries to agree on a particular organizational alternative. A review with the executive team is again in order. Modifications to the alternative are made again in preparation for a presentation at the final meeting.

Feedback to the Organization

The final meeting is usually a day and a half or two days long and includes the top three levels of the organization and other key contributors. Between fifty and eighty people are usually present. These are the people who will be affected by any changes. These are also the people who were exposed to the initial presentation and interviewed about the proposed alternatives. The purpose of the session is to update them on the design progress and to get their input one more time before committing to a particular design alternative.

The design team presents its analysis of the strategy and of the organization, the knowledge it gained during the process, its design criteria, and the recommended organizational alternative. After questions and answers, the group is broken into subgroups. Each subgroup is a cross section of the company. The subgroups are usually carefully designed to get a good balance of constituencies and personalities. A member of the design team is assigned to each group to answer questions. Facilitators can also be used.

The task of each subgroup is to critique the proposed alternative. If a group member disagrees with a portion of the proposed design, he or she must propose an alternative that meets the design criteria and then convince the other subgroup members. This process forces the subgroups to live with the general manager's problem and to act responsibly in making counterproposals. In this manner, the organization's members learn the strategy and the logic of the proposed organization. Their opinion is sought, heard, and used to modify alternatives before a final announcement is made.

Each subgroup meets for a half to a full day to reach its recommendation. The recommendations are made to the executive team at the end of the final meeting. The executive team and the general manager make their decision at this time, or shortly thereafter, based on the input of the organization.

Variations on the Design

There are variations in the design of the subgroups at the final meeting. Usually all groups get the same mission—to recommend an alternative for the entire organization. Sometimes, if an organization spans very large regions, two final meetings can be held, one in each region with cross-population of people from all of them. For example, one company had a meeting in Europe with some North Americans attending and another meeting in the United States with some Europeans attending. In this case, the organizations for Europe and North America were to be different, so the meeting in Europe naturally focused more on the European organization. Also, the organization was too complex to analyze as a whole. So different subgroups were given different portions of the design to look at. For example, two subgroups included predominantly members from back end, the manufacturing/engineering side of the organization. Their task was to concentrate on the proposed structure for this area. In this way, people with pertinent information can have more say in the changes that affect them directly.

Other Design Process Issues

Using this design process increases the probability that a strategic fit will be obtained and that the people whose cooperation is needed to implement the design are kept informed and supportive. Of course, some people will still be skeptical, but no process is 100 percent effective. However, this process produces a higher probability of success in building commitment.

There are always some standard questions. "What will keep the organization from coming to a stop while the design process is taking place?" is one. The answer is that the organization does not come to a stop, but people do invest energy in lobbying for their preferred outcomes. Any time a reorganization is contemplated, such lobbying discussions will take place. The described process tries to get the discussions out on the table rather than behind closed doors. It gives people a chance to object before a change is made. If their opinions are not sought and heard beforehand, they will express them afterward as "pocket vetoes" or through passive resistance. It's like the expression, "You pay me now or pay me later!" The time to design and implement a change is shorter when objections are sought and responded to before making the change. This process invests more up-front design time and in doing so reduces the amount of implementation time.

Like any management process, the design process improves with experience. The first time is the toughest. But with repeated use, an organizational facility with it will increase. With the need for frequent and rapid change, skill at the design process becomes an advantage.

Another issue that will affect the process is the organization's trust in management. A frequently asked question is, "How does the organization know that management has not already decided on an alternative? This process could be seen as just a charade." This question is a good one. Management must train itself not to decide prematurely and to listen to new information. By listening and modifying alternatives, management can show good faith and earn trust. Over time, the organization will see the process as an opportunity to learn and to influence change.

Of course, if management decides the outcome ahead of time and uses this process to sell its decision, it will be put in the worst of both cases. It will have invested valuable management time in the design process and still meet with resistance after the new organization structure is announced. The design process outlined here will not serve any management that the organization does not trust. However, for a management team that is trustworthy, the process is an opportunity to earn the trust and even the admiration of the organization members.

The design process provides a thorough method of collecting quality information for a good strategic fit. It provides ample opportunities for affected parties to influence the outcome. Finally, it helps to build commitment within the organization for the implementation of change. Both fit and commitment are required for an organizational design to be effective.

Conclusion

This book has tried to present a balanced and current analysis of organizational design. The position taken here has been that companies should choose among alternative organizations based on how well they meet criteria derived from the company's business strategy, rather than by how fashionable they are. Some companies in business situations characterized by extremes of variety, change, and speed may well find that the fashionable alternatives meet their criteria. But others may not. The important point is to choose what is effective, not what is attractive.

The book presented a number of the current organizational models, including the process organization, the distributed organization, the virtual corporation, and the front/back organizational model. In each case, I tried to identify the forces favoring—and those hindering—its choice. Also in each case I tried to present a complete design. That is, the star model gave a checklist of factors to be considered when designing an organization. The concept of alignment was introduced to use as a guide in choosing specific policies.

In conclusion, I wish to emphasize once again the role of leader. I see the leader as a *decision shaper* rather than a *decision maker*. The decision-shaping role is achieved through the organizational design. The star model provides the management-controlled policies that will influence how others make decisions.

References

Cohen, S. G. "Teams and Teamworks: Future Directions." In Galbraith and Lawler (eds.), *The Future of Organizations*. San Francisco: Jossey-Bass, 1993.

Detourzos, M. L., and Lester, R. K. *Made in America: Regaining the Productive Edge*. Cambridge, Mass.: MIT Press, 1989.

Dyer, W. G. *Team Building: Issues and Alternatives*. Reading, Mass.: Addison-Wesley, 1988.

Galbraith, J. "Designing the Innovating Organization," *Organization Dynamics*, 1982.

Galbraith, J. *Competing with Flexible Lateral Organizations*. (2nd ed.) Reading, Mass.: Addison-Wesley, 1994.

Lawler, E. E. *High-Involvement Management*. San Francisco: Jossey-Bass. 1986.

Lawler, E. E. *Strategic Pay: Aligning Organization Strategies and Pay Systems*. San Francisco: Jossey-Bass, 1990.

Lawler, E. E. *The Ultimate Advantage*. San Francisco: Jossey-Bass, 1992.

Mohrman, S. A., and Cummings, T. *Self Designing Organizations*. Reading, Mass.: Addison-Wesley, 1989.

"R&D Scoreboard," *Business Week*, June 1992.

Smith, D., and Katzenbach, J. *The Wisdom of Teams*. Boston: Harvard Business School Press, 1992.

Index